Are Markets Moral?

Are Markets Moral?

Edited by

Edward Skidelsky
Lecturer, University of Exeter, UK

and

Robert Skidelsky
Emeritus Professor of Political Economy,
University of Warwick, UK

Selection, introduction and editorial matter © Edward Skidelsky and Robert Skidelsky 2015

Individual chapters © contributors 2015

All rights reserved. No reproduction, copy or transmission of this publication may be made without written permission.

No portion of this publication may be reproduced, copied or transmitted save with written permission or in accordance with the provisions of the Copyright, Designs and Patents Act 1988, or under the terms of any licence permitting limited copying issued by the Copyright Licensing Agency, Saffron House, 6–10 Kirby Street, London EC1N 8TS.

Any person who does any unauthorised act in relation to this publication may be liable to criminal prosecution and civil claims for damages.

The authors have asserted their rights to be identified as the authors of this work in accordance with the Copyright, Designs and Patents Act 1988.

First published 2015 by
PALGRAVE MACMILLAN

Palgrave Macmillan in the UK is an imprint of Macmillan Publishers Limited, registered in England, company number 785998, of Houndmills, Basingstoke, Hampshire RG21 6XS.

Palgrave Macmillan in the US is a division of St Martin's Press LLC, 175 Fifth Avenue, New York, NY 10010.

Palgrave Macmillan is the global academic imprint of the above companies and has companies and representatives throughout the world.

Palgrave® and Macmillan® are registered trademarks in the United States, the United Kingdom, Europe and other countries.

ISBN 978–1–137–47273–1

This book is printed on paper suitable for recycling and made from fully managed and sustained forest sources. Logging, pulping and manufacturing processes are expected to conform to the environmental regulations of the country of origin.

A catalogue record for this book is available from the British Library.

A catalog record for this book is available from the Library of Congress.

Typeset by MPS Limited, Chennai, India.

Contents

Preface and Acknowledgement	vi
Notes on the Contributors	vii
Introduction	1
Session 1: Restraining Insatiability	**8**
Robert Skidelsky	8
Perry Anderson	15
Robert H. Frank	21
Discussion	32
Session 2: Equality and Corruption	**44**
Steven Lukes	44
Glen Newey	55
Discussion	65
Session 3: The Moral Limits of Markets	**77**
Edward Skidelsky	77
John Milbank	86
Discussion	96
Session 4: The Meaning of Money	**103**
Felix Martin	103
Geoffrey Hosking	117
David Graeber	125
Discussion	137
Index	145

Preface and Acknowledgement

The symposium 'Markets and Morals' took place over four sessions in London on 23 May 2013. Transcripts were made of the presentations and the discussion to which they gave rise. What the editors have done here is to reproduce the corrected presentations and give a flavour of the discussion.

We would like to thank: the House of Lords for making the conference room available and for providing refreshments; the Centre for Global Studies (CGS), which made the symposium financially possible; Nan Craig and Pete Mills of CGS, who handled the logistics; Ubiqus, for transcription services; and of course all those who attended, either as main speakers or discussants.

EDWARD and ROBERT SKIDELSKY

Acknowledgement: the material on pages 117 to 125 draws on material from Chapter 4 'Money: Creator and Destroyer of Trust' in *Trust: A History* by Geoffrey Hosking (2014) by permission of Oxford University Press.

Notes on the Contributors

Showkat Ali is a PhD student in philosophy at University College London, UK. His research interests are in ethics and political philosophy, in particular consequentialism, non-consequentialism, equality and distributive justice.

Perry Anderson is one of the most influential figures on the intellectual Left. He is Professor of History and Sociology at the University of California, Los Angeles (UCLA), USA, and a former editor of the *New Left Review*. His books are seminal contributions to political theory and include, among others, *Spectrum*, *Lineages of the Absolutist State*, *Passages from Antiquity to Feudalism*, *Considerations on Western Marxism*, *English Questions*, *The Origins of Postmodernity*, *The Indian Ideology*, and most recently *American Foreign Policy and Its Thinkers*.

Philip Blond founded ResPublica in 2009 and is an academic, journalist and author. Prior to entering politics and public policy he was Senior Lecturer in Theology and Philosophy – teaching at the Universities of Exeter and Cumbria in the UK. He is the author of *Red Tory* (2010), which sought to redefine the centre-ground of British politics around the ideas of civil association, mutual ownership and shared enterprise. His ideas have influenced the agenda around the Big Society and civil renewal and have helped to redefine British and international politics. He has written extensively in the British and foreign press including the *Guardian*, the *Independent*, the *Observer*, *The Financial Times*, *Prospect*, the *New Statesman* and *The New York Times*.

viii *Notes on the Contributors*

Richard Bronk is a writer and part-time academic, with particular expertise in the history of ideas, the philosophy of economics, comparative corporate governance and European political economy. Educated at Merton College, Oxford, he then spent seventeen years in the City of London. Between 2000 to 2007 he was a Teaching Fellow at the European Institute, London School of Economics and Political Science, UK. Since 2007 he has been a Visiting Fellow at the Institute. Richard is also a Fellow of the Royal Society of Arts. His research interests centre on the role of imagination, language and metaphor in economics, the dangers of economic monoculture and the epistemology of markets. He is author of *Progress and the Invisible Hand: The Philosophy and Economics of Human Advance* (1998) and *The Romantic Economist: Imagination in Economics* (2009).

Nan Craig is Programmes and Publications Director at the Centre for Global Studies, a think-tank that aims to publish work on economics that reflects a broad, pluralistic approach. She has written fiction and non-fiction for the *New Statesman*, *Arc* magazine and the *New Internationalist*.

Jonathan Derbyshire is Managing Editor of *Prospect* magazine. He was formerly Culture Editor of the *New Statesman*. His literary journalism has also appeared in the *Daily Telegraph*, *The Financial Times*, the *Guardian*, the *New York Sun*, *Prospect*, *The Times Literary Supplement* and *Time Out*. In 2007 he edited *Time Out: 1000 Books to Change Your Life*. He has also written reviews for *The Philosophers' Magazine* and *New Humanist*.

Robert H. Frank is the Henrietta Johnson Louis Professor of Management and Professor of Economics at Cornell University's Johnson Graduate School of Management and the co-director of the Paduano Seminar in Business Ethics at New York University's Stern School of Business, USA. His 'Economic View' column appears monthly in *The New York Times*. He is a Distinguished Senior Fellow at Demos. *The Winner-Take-All Society*, co-authored with Philip Cook, received a Critic's Choice Award, was named a Notable Book of the Year by *The New York Times*, and was included in *Business Week*'s list of the ten best books of 1995. He is a co-recipient of the 2004 Leontief Prize for Advancing the Frontiers of Economic Thought.

David Graeber is an American anthropologist, author and activist who is Professor of Anthropology at the London School of Economics and Political Science and was previously Reader in Social Anthropology at Goldsmiths, University of London, UK, and Associate Professor of Anthropology at Yale University in the USA. He is the author of several books, including *Debt: The First 5,000 Years* (2011) and most recently *The Democracy Project* (2013).

Geoffrey Hosking is a British historian of Russia and the Soviet Union and formerly Leverhulme Research Professor of Russian History at the School of Slavonic and East European Studies (SSEES) at University College London, UK. He is the author of the award-winning *History of the Soviet Union* and most recently of *Trust: A History* (2014).

Steven Lukes is Professor of Sociology at New York University in the USA and the author of numerous books and articles about political and social theory, including his best-known and still controversial theory of power: *Power: A Radical View*. He was formerly a fellow at Balliol College, Oxford, and has taught at the European University Institute, Florence, and the University of

Siena in Italy and at the London School of Economics and Political Science in the UK. He is a member of the editorial board of the *European Journal of Sociology* and a fellow of the British Academy.

Felix Martin is a macroeconomist and bond investor. He was educated in the UK, Italy and the US, where he was a Fulbright scholar; and has degrees in classics, international relations and economics. He worked at the World Bank from 1998 to 2008, mostly on the reconstruction of the former Yugoslavia, and since 2008 he has worked in the fund management industry in London. He is an associate of the Institute for New Economic Thinking in New York, and of the Centre for Global Studies in London. His writing has appeared in the *New York Review of Books*, *Wired*, *The Financial Times* and the *Guardian*; he also writes the 'Real Money' column for the *New Statesman*. His first book, *Money: The Unauthorised Biography*, was published in June 2013.

John Milbank is Professor of Religion, Politics and Ethics at the University of Nottingham, UK, where he also directs the Centre of Theology and Philosophy. He previously taught at the University of Virginia in the USA and before that in the UK at the University of Cambridge and the University of Lancaster, and is the author of several books, including *Theology and Social Theory* (1991) and most recently *Being Reconciled: Ontology and Pardon* (2003). He was also one of the editors of the *Radical Orthodoxy: A New Theology* (1998).

Véronique Munoz-Dardé is Professor of Philosophy at University College London, UK. Her main interests lie in moral and political philosophy. She has written articles on the importance of numbers in practical reasoning, on the political ideal of equality, on responsibility and on distributive justice. She is the author of *La justice sociale* (2001) and is currently finishing a book called *Bound Together: Claims of Others and the Needs of Selves*. She is also writing a 'Guidebook to Rawls' and *A Theory of Justice*. Since 2009 she has been in residence at University of California, Berkeley, USA, each year in the Fall semester.

Glen Newey is Professor of Practical Philosophy in the Institute for Philosophy at the University of Leiden, Netherlands, and is the author of *Hobbes and Leviathan* (2007), *After Politics* (2001) and *Virtue, Reason and Toleration: The Place of Toleration in Ethical and Political Philosophy* (1999). He is a frequent reviewer and commentator for the *London Review of Books*, *The Independent*, the *New Statesman* and *The Times Literary Supplement*.

Richard Seaford is Professor of the Department of Classics and Ancient History at the University of Exeter, UK. His recent books include *Money and the Early Greek Mind: Homer, Philosophy, Tragedy* (2004) on the development of Greek culture in the sixth century BC and its connection to monetisation, exploring the socio-historical conditions that made this first monetisation possible as well as its profound cultural consequences, notably the invention of 'philosophy' and of drama. He is also the author of *Cosmology and the Polis: The Social Construction of Space and Time in the Tragedies of Aeschylus* (2012). For the period 2005–8 he was awarded a Leverhulme Major Research Fellowship by the Leverhulme Trust. For 2013–14 he was awarded an Arts and Humanities Research Council Fellowship for a comparative historical study of early Indian with early Greek thought.

Edward Skidelsky is Lecturer in Philosophy at the University of Exeter in the UK and the author of *Ernst Cassirer: The Last Philosopher of Culture* and, with Robert

Skidelsky, *How Much Is Enough? The Love of Money and the Case for the Good Life* (2012). He has written regularly for the *Guardian* and *Prospect*.

Robert Skidelsky is Emeritus Professor of Political Economy at Warwick University, UK. His three-volume biography of John Maynard Keynes (1983, 1992, 2000) won five prizes and his book on the financial crisis – *Keynes: The Return of the Master* – was published in September 2010. He was made a member of the House of Lords in 1991 (he sits on the cross-benches) and elected a fellow of the British Academy in 1994. *How Much Is Enough? The Love of Money and the Case for the Good Life*, co-written with his son Edward, was published in 2012. His most recent book is *Britain since 1900: A Success Story?* (2014).

Introduction

The theme of the symposium was about what happens to the morality of a society in which money rules the roost – that is, a society in which exchanges between people increasingly take the form of buying and selling goods and services for money. This is the society in which we live.

We should admit a bias straight away: the topics and speakers were selected to highlight what is wrong with markets rather than what is right with them. However, capitalist market society – the only form in which market society has existed – has always been praised more for its efficiency and dynamism than for its morality. Its morality is commonly held to be imported from outside – from religion or from custom. It was Schumpeter who suggested that capitalism was bound to undermine the moral foundations on which it depended.[1] The symposium was an exploration of this idea.

For Robert and Edward Skidelsky, the stimulus to organise this event was the publication, the previous summer, of their book *How Much Is Enough?*,[2] which advocated curbs on acquisitiveness. Capitalism's encouragement of greed is frequently considered to be its main moral failing, while also being the source of its economic energy. The background to the symposium was the financial collapse of 2008–09, which for many seemed the nemesis of a greedy capitalism freed from moral restraints. But the symposium was not solely, or even mainly, about the 'greed' of capitalism. A major theme was the contamination of moral values, including those of security and equality, by money values. Instead of the market being embedded in society, society has come to be embedded in the market. The business of modern society is business. This has moral consequences.

The first session, 'Restraining Insatiability', raised the following questions. Are the sources of insatiability inborn or social? Does insatiability today attach more to money or goods? And what forces of change ('agency') might exist, or be brought into existence, to reverse its onward march?

Robert H. Frank denied that insatiability is inborn. What *is* 'hard-wired' into individuals is the desire for improvement. But what counts as improvement depends on social context – the 'frame of reference'. When context matters, relative income matters. Large income inequalities are inefficient, because they divert spending into competitive consumption. To curb this Frank advocated a progressive consumption tax. Discussants agreed that insatiability is a matter of social context rather than 'original sin'. According to Richard Seaford, 'acquisitive individualism' entered history with the invention of money. Felix Martin agreed: it was money which made static societies dynamic.

Robert Skidelsky suggested that in modern capitalism accumulation of money has become the true insatiability, because of its fungibility. Perry Anderson doubted that 'sheer love of money disfigures more than a very narrow stratum at the top of our hugely – and increasingly – unequal societies. Pursuit of goods strikes me still as much more widespread than the accumulation of money'. He went on to ask who or what would be the agents for the reforms the Skidelskys and Frank advocated.

Three views emerged. They are, roughly, the religious, the political and the technocratic. John Milbank thought that we have to reinvent moral agency. Perry Anderson looked to 'social actors', modern equivalents of the old labour movement. Robert H. Frank thought that economic persuasion, plus a bill in Congress, could readily deliver his progressive consumption tax. However, catastrophe is the joker in the pack: the current reforms of the banking system have clearly been driven by the financial excesses which led to the collapse of 2008. But what effect will they have in diverting financial practice from its predatory course?

Steven Lukes opened the next session, 'Equality and Corruption', by distinguishing between two possible moral harms wrought by a marketised society: the intrinsic and the aggravating. The first is said to arise from buying and selling as such; the second is largely a function of inequality in market relations. Lukes thought that the first type of harm – the corruption of a practice or social relation by subjecting it to monetary evaluation – had been greatly exaggerated by writers like Michael Sandel; in all societies, money relations were intertwined with intimate ones. On the other hand, prostitution was an example of an aggravating harm. In theory, the buying and selling of sex was no more noxious than the buying and selling of any service; in practice prostitution signified and perpetuated the inequality of women.

Glen Newey agreed with Lukes that inequality of market position rather than marketisation in itself was the moral flaw of capitalist society. Consider the case of buying and selling votes. In principle, it promises a Pareto-superior outcome: those who don't bother to vote would receive a cash payment; those buying votes would be in a better position to influence policy. In practice, those who buy votes are bound to have superior market power to those who sell them, thus skewing political outcomes in favour of the rich. Newey observed that this was not completely unlike the way our modern voting systems actually work (money talks loudest); he echoed Lukes in warning against accepting the economists' picture of idealised markets, which abstracted from power. In depicting the moral failures of markets as largely deriving from a (correctible) inequality of market position, Lukes and Newey argued from a well-trodden social democratic tradition.

Discussion centred on: problems for public policy arising from the incommensurability of values; the nature of the case against buying and selling votes; and whether the contamination involved in monetising a practice was intrinsic or only contingent (and the distinction between these two). Newey and Martin argued against Robert Seaford that a Benthamite calculus – reducing the incommensurable to the commensurable – was needed for the purposes of public policy, even though the cost–benefit calculus was bound to be partly fictional.

According to Newey, the core of the case against buying and selling votes was incommensurability of values, and consequently the need for a democratic counterweight to the power of the rich; David Graeber agreed that 'politics is the art of mediating publicly between incommensurable values at the social level'. For Frank, the big argument against monetising votes was not value conflict but the free-rider problem: in a large electorate, those who sell their votes to a polluter on the assumption that others will vote against may create a worse outcome for all.

Finally, is the marketing of education and medicine inherently or only contingently bad? According to Seaford, 'most people would say the goal of doctoring is health and if it is diminished by money-making so much the worse for money-making ... Aristotle deals precisely with this issue'. To which Newey responded that 'it is going to be quite hard to justify public policy outcomes by reference to the fourfold typology of *teloi* in Aristotle'.

In the third session, on 'The Moral Limits of Markets', Edward Skidelsky picked up the Aristotelian baton. He argued that marketisation of many practices is immoral per se, because it perverts the internal goals of the practice or activity. Thus prostitution is morally harmful, not just contingently, as Lukes suggested, but inherently, by destroying the purpose of sexual activity, which is the expression of reciprocal desire. Prostitution is an example of the prostitution of an internal goal for the sake of money, in the same way as 'schmoctoring' (selling medical services for money) perverts the internal goal of doctoring.

John Milbank explained how the 'marketplace', which is a normal part of the exchange system of any society, which can operate to fixed moral conventions and hierarchies, has been crowded out in the course of capitalist evolution by the 'market', where goods and services are exchanged according to the laws of supply and demand. He argued that the development of the capitalist model of economy was not inevitable, but an unintended effect of the Christian (particularly Jansenist) belief in original sin. This came to be coupled with the view that divine Providence creates order through our vices, not virtues, a view taken over in naturalistic form by Adam Smith. The task is not to equalise market exchanges but to re-embed economy in society, which he saw as the task of a new socialism.

Two topics dominated the discussion which followed. The first concerned the nature of sexual corruption. Newey wondered whether a loveless couple which stays together for the purpose of procreation represents a perversion of sex, in Edward Skidelsky's terms. Nan Craig asked whether prostitutes who provide sexual services for people with severe disabilities are undermining the telos of sex. The second debate concerned the nature of 'corporate social responsibility'. Frank claimed that many companies aim to make money by keeping their customers and employees happy; Milbank dismissed Harvard

Business School arguments for social responsibility as a kind of window-dressing.

The last session, on 'The Meaning of Money', featured Felix Martin, Geoffrey Hosking and David Graeber. All three rejected the view that money has any value in itself; its function is to shape the values of society, to regulate social relations. Martin called it a 'social technology', Graeber a 'moral technology'. Dollars, pounds and euros, said Martin, were simply 'units of measurement of an abstract scale of values'. This scale was 'intrinsically social'. Any attempt to 'fix' the price of money was as futile as trying to fix the quantity of words in a language. However, the state had an enormous influence on the value of money, and hence on the social structure. Insofar as excessive debt was the overriding problem of contemporary economies, the remedy was simple: the state could inflate away the debt, and thus restore a proper balance between creditors and debtors.

Graeber offered a fascinating historical survey of the shifting relationship between creditors and debtors over time. He pointed out that all the world religions believe that morality is a matter of paying one's debts. But this put political power into the hands of the creditor class, and hence led to debtors' revolts. Eras of commodity money, in which creditors dominate, give way to eras of credit money, which favour debtors. Underpinning the commodity view of money is an insistence on the moral value of work. These two moralities – the morality of paying one's debts and the morality of work – represent the main moral underpinnings of contemporary capitalism. But, like Schumpeter, Graeber sees a contradiction between the long-term interests of the system – which is regular debt relief and reduction in work hours – and the moral mechanisms legitimising it.

For Geoffrey Hosking, money is a 'symbol of trust'. His contention was that 'the function of money is to fix the human predisposition to trust and make it effective economically'. Without what he calls 'a strong thin trust', an extended society and economy would be impossible. However, when money is not a mediator of trust, it becomes a powerful mediator of distrust. That is why unregulated markets generate booms and busts which dislocate entire economies. A second problem with money is that it is disconnected from other symbolic systems. Those engaged in the business of money assume they are emancipated from ethics, from religion and even from the law. Echoing Lukes and the Skidelskys, Hosking concludes that money 'possesses dangerous powers which can undermine, colonise and degrade what in life we would otherwise cherish'.

Three issues were raised in the discussion. First, what caused the cycles of creditor and debtor ascendancy? David Graeber suggested that they were associated with the state of military technology, particularly the rise and fall of professional armies. Second, Perry Anderson wondered whether Martin's inflationary remedy for debt would not destroy the trust which Hosking looked for in money. Third, what might be the historical mechanisms for preventing debt accumulation, like the usury laws and caps, and what might be their modern equivalents?

Notes

1. J.A. Schumpeter, *Capitalism, Socialism and Democracy*, 3rd edn (New York: Harper & Row, 1950).
2. R. Skidelsky and E. Skidelsky, *How Much is Enough? The Love of Money and the Case for the Good Life* (London: Allen Lane, 2012).

Session 1

Restraining Insatiability

Robert Skidelsky

My interest in insatiability was triggered off by Keynes's prediction in 1930 that 100 years hence people in rich countries would have enough, and therefore work less. This was based on an assumption about productivity growth. That prediction turned out to be partly wrong. Although average incomes have risen, much in line with Keynes's prediction, average hours of work have fallen much less. This suggested that he underestimated human insatiability. My son Edward and I wrote a book called *How Much Is Enough?*, which was an inquiry into the meaning and causes of insatiability. This is a further exploration of that topic, which suggests one or two modifications of the view we took in the book.

The dictionary definition of 'insatiable' is, not surprisingly, 'not satiable', that which cannot be appeased and which always craves for more. In economic life, we can think of two sources of insatiability: love of goods and love of money. The question is, really, which is the more important? Which is the driver of the system we now have? Conventional economics only recognises one source of insatiability: the love of goods. It treats money simply as a means to satisfy our wants, while recognising that our wants may be insatiable. Money as such has no utility. Desire for money as an end is irrational and needs special psychological explanation. We know that there is the psychology of the miser, who is someone who loves money for its own sake, but that is regarded as a species of disease.

I want to put forward an alternative hypothesis, which is that the true insatiability – the insatiability that knows no limits at all – is love of money, not love of goods. My hypothesis is that the marginal utility of goods shows a tendency to decline, whereas the marginal utility of money shows no such tendency. This is because love of goods comes up against the limits of use and usefulness, whereas money contains all the imaginable possibilities for use without requiring a decision about spending it. It is an imagined world, with no reality check. Schopenhauer calls it 'frozen desire', which is also the title of a fine book by James Buchan.[1] The deepest thinkers about money have long recognised its power to transform itself from means to an end, and – in the extreme – to crowd out all other ends. There is the legend of King Midas: everything that he touched, including food, turned to gold, and therefore he starved to death.

In King Midas's day, money was gold, and the legend only makes sense in a world of commodity money. One had to dig for gold; and digging for gold was at the expense of digging for food. There was an absolute limit placed on the accumulation of money: the opportunity cost of starving to death. In a world of fiat money there is no limit to the amount of it that can be created. The desire for money can therefore expand without limit: all the central bank has to do is to print the stuff. No one in today's world need suffer King Midas's fate. The accumulation of money has lost its economic sting.

There is a strong argument that the recent economic crisis was a crisis of love of money. The frenzied pursuit of money by the financial system carried us to a pinnacle of fake wealth, far above any concrete utility; when its production temporarily froze, the temple came crashing down. Now attempts are under way to reboot the economy by pumping up the money supply. It follows from this that any attempt to curb insatiability must start with taming money, with re-establishing it as a means, and making it more difficult – legally and morally – to accumulate as an end. It is only secondarily that we need to find ways of reducing the hunger for goods. That somewhat reverses the emphasis of our book, in which we argued that hunger for goods was the thing that needed to be restrained. I am just putting this forward as a hypothesis: I am not committed to saying that one is more important than the other.

Let us start at the opposite end with the urge to consume, treating money simply as a facilitator of this. It is hardly surprising that economics started from this point, because work was the effort needed to wrest a living from the soil. 'The end of production is consumption' said Adam Smith. Money was a bit player in this struggle for consumption. It appears in economics simply as a means of exchange, which allowed a larger variety of goods to be consumed from the same output. Psychological and spiritual insatiability was recognised always to be there, but I think it was in some way regarded as derivative of physical need: as in greed for food. Economics has always accepted the materialist theory of history.

The invention of credit – which dates from as early as 3000BC – alerted thinkers of antiquity to the possibility that money could be detached from need; that it could, in fact, breed itself. Hence Aristotle's ban on usury: charging interest for the loan of money. That ban ruled throughout the Middle Ages, was only gradually lifted in the West and is still the official law of Islam. Money's natural purpose, Aristotle held, was to acquire the good things of life. If it was used to breed itself, it was an unnatural vice, like sleeping with one's mother. Dante placed usurers and sodomites, both violators of nature, in the seventh circle of hell.

Then you have the idea in Gibbon in the 18th century that money gives more active energy to the powers and passions of human nature: that is, it quickens the growth of wealth, but does not supersede the purpose of wealth creation, which was to expand consumption. In the Gibbon/Smith story of early economics the desire for money is simply a desire for the goods money will buy, both for oneself and others. That is how I interpret it, anyway.

However, Smith has already blurred the distinction between needs and wants. Aristotle's natural needs become Smith's natural desire for improvement – a kind of divine restlessness – and so the physical yields to the psychological. Money's role in releasing and satisfying restlessness is a standard defence of the role of money, because it liberates people from old restrictions. Here is Jevons on the hierarchy of wants: 'The necessaries of life are so few and simple that a man is soon dissatisfied in regard to these, and desires to extend the range of enjoyment. His first object is to vary his food, but there soon arises the desire of variety and elegance in dress, and to this succeeds the desire to build, to ornament, and to furnish; tastes which – where they exist – are absolutely insatiable, and seem to increase with every improvement in civilisation.' This is the continuation of the Smith view of an inborn desire for improved quality, which is quickened by a money economy.

I would query Jevons's use of the word 'insatiable', because by a 'hierarchy of wants', which is what he is describing, he means to say – and I quote – 'that the satisfaction of every lower want in the scale created a desire of a higher character ... The highest grade in the scale of wants, that of pleasure derived from the beauties of nature and art, is usually confined to men who are exempted from all lower privations.' That, to me, does not suggest a progression from a limited amount of gadgets to a huge number of gadgets, but rather from lower to higher wants, from the material to the aesthetic. Jevons's idea of a hierarchy is actually very close to Keynes's idea in *Economic Possibilities for our Grandchildren*,[2] where we progress from the material to the spiritual.

We then move on. In our book, Edward and I take up the analysis of insatiability as left by Jevons and his generation. In his book, *The Joyless Economy*, the economist Tibor Scitovsky provided a psychological underpinning for Smith's urge to improvement. His main idea is that every novelty leaves one unsatisfied, creating the urge for further novelty, and he posits a psychological addiction to novelty, which has a physical basis like any other addiction. Every pleasure leaves you dissatisfied, so you want more and more. There is no progress in Scitovsky from lower to higher pleasures: with technological progress a virtually unlimited supply of novelty is available to feed jaded appetites. Scitovsky, like Galbraith, also highlights the role of advertising in provoking restlessness and producing more desire.

The economist's explanation of insatiability for goods starts, then, with individual restlessness. There is a sociological tradition, though, whose starting point is the idea that wants are insatiable because they are relative. In this account, insatiability is not driven by an inborn individual restlessness, but by a constant process of comparison with others. Veblen's theory of conspicuous consumption is the most famous of these contextual theories of insatiability.

Both the economic and the sociological accounts of insatiability see it as attaching to love of goods. I want to query this, because I think the desire for more goods is not limitless. Goods are bought for use, even if the only use is display. Although you can extend the use and the variety of goods almost without limit, you cannot extend it without limit. Ultimately you run up against the opportunity cost of novelty: its cost in terms of other desired goals. I suspect that the desire for novelty would have come into conflict with other objects of human striving much sooner but for money.

So we turn to money. Veblen grasped the truth of money's exemption from the law of diminishing marginal utility. Here, he puts it rather graphically, in a remarkable essay called *The Limits of Marginal Utility*, 'the hedonistically presumed final purchase of consumable goods is habitually not contemplated in the pursuit of business enterprise. Businessmen habitually aspire to accumulate wealth in excess of the limits of practicable consumption, and the wealth so accumulated is not intended to be converted by a final transaction of purchase into consumable goods or sensations of consumption.' Here is the theorist of conspicuous consumption saying that businessmen accumulate far in excess of what they want to consume, now or later. For them there is no hedonic treadmill. Let us pursue this.

Like Aristotle, Marx noticed the dual aspect of money, both as a means and an end, and summed it up in the French proverb, *'L'argent n'a pas de maître'*. On the one hand, money was a means of liberation from feudalism – it liberated you from other masters – but, on the other hand, money has no master. In other words, it is the master. Quoting Goethe but echoing Aristotle, Marx wrote of money that it comes to have 'love in its body'; he pointed out that, under the capitalist division of labour, the interests of consumption and accumulation were severed from each other. Labour as a commodity works to earn money to buy commodities for consumption – that is, goods – which Marx represented in the formula C-M-C'. But the capitalist parts with money to buy labour to make more money – M-C-M' – the excess of M over M' being the source of Marx's surplus value. The accumulation of money is thus the dominant motive for business activity. Whether the capitalist also consumes conspicuously is irrelevant. Victorian businessmen were, on the whole, quite frugal in their habits.

Of course, Marx regarded surplus value as the source of business crises, gradually increasing in intensity. For the full system of labour exploitation to be established, money had to dethrone the traditional gods, and the splendid passage in *The Communist Manifesto* depicting the replacement of traditional social ties by the cash nexus was foreshadowed by Marx's favoured passage from Shakespeare's *Timon of Athens*, where Timon addresses a heap of gold he has dug up: 'Thus much of this will make black white, foul fair / Wrong right, base noble, old young, coward valiant.' 'This yellow slave / Will knit and break religions.'

This testifies to the idea of the overwhelming power of money to transform, disrupt and destroy all social relations. You start thinking of it as a slave and you end up by worshipping it. It stimulates the passion for money itself, because money promises the power to fulfil all other passions. Keynes follows exactly this. He says, 'the test of money measurement constantly tends to widen the area where we weigh concrete goods against abstract money. Our imaginations are too weak for the choice. Abstract money outweighs them. We want to diminish, rather than increase, the area of monetary comparison.' Well, we have gone the other way.

So to conclude. Aristotle thinks only of natural need, but there is no limit to human desire. The hypothesis I have been advancing suggests that only by restricting the domain of money can human desire be prevented from limitless expansion. The way to restrict the domain of money is by restricting the rewards which attach to the accumulation of money. The principle would be to tax all accumulations not spent on consumption or adding to capital equipment.

That is what this line of thought leads one to, but the line of thought in our book was slightly different. We wanted to tax objects of consumption, because our idea was that insatiability had its root in the love of goods. So which view does one take? Perhaps the answer depends on where one looks. Households consume; businesses accumulate. The financial corporation, which is the dominant institution of modern capitalism, embodies the urge to accumulate in its pure form. My tentative hypothesis is that love of money is much the most disruptive force in present-day society and if one can, to some extent, demonetise the economy, that will simultaneously restore some of the traditional barriers to excessive consumption.

Perry Anderson

Let me express at the outset my admiration for the book – which I am sure you have all read – written by Robert and Edward, *How Much Is Enough?*, which is a powerful, elegant and level-headed work containing both a critique of the addiction to growth in the rich countries of the world and a set of proposals of how to check it. It gives us both a diagnosis and a remedy.

Our average incomes have increased nearly as much as Keynes thought they would three-quarters of a century ago, but the hours we work have not declined by anything like the amount that he expected, and there is little or no evidence that happiness has increased along with wealth.

Moreover, current attempts to estimate subjective levels of wellbeing are, in their eyes, a mis-measure of their object, since not happiness conceived in any utilitarian mode but a good life is the proper goal of social thought and action. This good life comprises many elements that are not measurable at all, alongside health, which is, and security, which is only doubtfully so. Respect, friendship, personality, harmony with nature, and genuine leisure – not mere recreation – are clearly not measurable in the same way.

To steer us away from our current conditions of growth addiction towards lives that might realise these goods, Robert and Edward urge a series of practical reforms in the book. These include: the introduction of a universal basic income, financed from transaction taxes and carbon credits; a progressive expenditure, rather than income tax; statutory reduction of working hours; and the disallowance of advertising as a business expense. In this session, Robert has somewhat modified both the diagnosis and the remedies set out in the book, arguing that it is not addiction to ever-newer and newer commodities but to money itself which is the addiction to be broken. In consequence, progressive taxation should focus on accumulation, not consumption, wherever there is no addition to capital stock.

He ends with some fascinating passages from Keynes. But I think it is fair to say that the spirit of his modification brings him in some ways closer to Marx's famous encapsulation of capital: 'Accumulate, accumulate! That is Moses and the prophets!' Of course, that is an injunction for capitalists specifically. Whether such an imperative is really society-wide, encompassing all classes, is a question we might press him on. I myself doubt that sheer love of money disfigures more than a very narrow stratum at the top of our hugely – and increasingly – unequal societies.

Pursuit of goods strikes me still as much more widespread than the accumulation of money, against which we should remember there exists, after all, a well-known and vast repertoire of popular warnings and, indeed, disdain – 'you can't take it with you', and the like. We could list many adages of that kind from popular wisdom.

However, Robert's alteration scarcely affects the structure and force of the argument of the book. There is, however, a gap in its argument, to which I want to address my remarks. It is this. Between the critique of the existing social or economic order and the vision of a better one, the issue of agency remains unaddressed. How concretely are we to get from 'Addicted', A, to 'Liberated', B? What forces or mechanisms might deliver the remedies outlined? Although these remedies are moderate in tone – the book is entirely free from any kind of Savonarola tone – it is enough to look at what is considered practical politics in all the advanced capitalist countries today to see that these remedies involve a radical transformation of existing social arrangements.

So how might this come about? Reading between the lines of *How Much Is Enough?*, one could perhaps glimpse four possibilities within its framework. These do not appear, however, directly as agencies, but in the guise – rather along Alasdair MacIntyre lines – of scattered shards of older social moralities, or perhaps some new ones. Of the former, Robert and Edward list the following: Catholic teaching that culminated in Christian democratic conceptions of the social market; Protestant New Liberalism of the Asquith era and its second wind with Keynes, Beveridge and FDR; and, finally, the somewhat more egalitarian version of liberalism in European social democracy.

Now, if you want to translate these fragments of morality into elements of a causal history, what we have are two quite distinct agencies. The first was the rise of the labour movements at the turn of the 20th century and the pressure of new working-class electorates on the political establishments of the time. Certainly, this could take the shape of the social reforms of New Liberalism in Britain, but it could also take the shape of Bismarckian social insurance or indeed, elsewhere, changes wrought directly by the social democratic parties themselves. In either case, however, I do not think it was so much moral distress at the plight of the poor that put reforms on the agenda – that had, after all, long pre-existed this period – as it was the organised strength of workers.

The second pattern which one can read between the lines here was quite distinct from this; namely, a response to the great economic crisis of the 1930s which produced Keynes's *General Theory*, Beveridge's Report and Roosevelt's New Deal. This was a second instalment of New Liberalism, but the immediate spur to it was the Great Depression, not the rise of labour as such. Here, the agency of change was economic emergency, rather than the appearance of a new social actor. As for Christian democracy, while it is true that German ordoliberalism can be traced back to the 1930s and Papal encyclicals on poverty and property much further back, the social market economy as an operative model in Germany really only dates from the late 1940s onwards. Its influence came, essentially, from the disaster of the Second World War. War, of course, was a prime factor in the release of the Beveridge Report.

Now, apart from the pressure of a new social actor and a traumatic economic shock, what other levers of potential historical change might we imagine as bearing some chance of the kind of transformation Robert and Edward envisage? Two further possibilities are latent in their text. The first is simply ecological catastrophe: natural disasters so great that they would bring growth addicts to their senses. However, in one of the most interesting chapters of *How Much Is Enough?*, Robert and Edward discount any apocalyptic theories of global warming, arguing that there is little reason to suppose that humans will not have developed technologies capable of dealing, in due course, with a three or four degree increase in global climates.

Lastly, however, in their final paragraphs, Robert and Edward suggest that a religious awakening could perhaps 'bring the necessary correction to our ways of living. Would such a reorientation of policy require the support of religion? It is possible. The basic goods, as we present them, are not logically dependent on any single doctrine, but their realisation is probably impossible without the authority and inspiration that only religion can provide'.

To recapitulate, then, formally speaking four alternative agencies capable of bringing growth addiction to an end could be deduced from *How Much Is Enough?* That is: new social actors emerging today, comparable to the labour movement of old; economic crises on the scale of the slump; the impact of global warming; and an upsurge of religious faith, maybe comparable to that of the dawn of Christianity. Two of these potential mechanisms are positive in character – social actors and religious beliefs – and two – economic slump and ecological disaster – are negative. I would challenge our authors to tell us somewhat more about what their view of each of these today would be.

To take the first: would the contemporary middle classes, whose global ascent and expansion is so much bruited in the media and elsewhere today, fit the bill as successors to the old working class as candidates for the role of new social actors; or, at any rate, those sections of the middle classes whom the Anglo-Italian historian

Paul Ginsborg has distinguished as *ceti medi riflessivi*, rather than *ceti medi rampanti*: the reflective, not merely the avaricious and consumerist, sections of the middle class?

To take the third of these scenarios, how far do the authors really dismiss the possibility of quite rapid ecological disasters striking major population centres in the shape of, for example, floods stemming from the melting of ice caps, before any technologies have been developed to avert or contain them? Or, to take the fourth, how plausible is an upsurge of religious faith in the rich societies today? Even in the United States – famously the homeland of one theological awakening after another – the proportion of non-believers is steadily increasing. About a quarter of the population disavows any Christianity. More generally, what do Robert and Edward think of Ernest Gellner's well-known thesis of the 'rubber cage': that is, his dismissal of factitious, spiritualised re-enchantments of the world that he thought were no barrier to rampant consumerism, but a logical complement to it?

Finally, what of economic setbacks much deeper than those we are now living through? Our authors, after all, write at one point that 'any radical shift in consciousness requires the stimulus of crisis'. Would not another slump represent the kind of shock that could reshuffle all the cards in the mental deck of well-off societies? Or do they judge that the modest adjustments now being made to the ruling models of the past 30 years constitute sufficient guarantee that nothing like this is ever likely to happen again? Our theme is markets and morals, but, of course, neither of these exists in a historical or political vacuum. *How Much Is Enough?* touches on the social landscape since the 1970s. The next task for its authors is to enlarge on that.

Robert H. Frank

I am often struck by how my thoughts have been shaped by people I have to argue with, and how my thinking might have evolved differently in the very different political climate of the UK. The moral legitimacy of the welfare state in Britain is more or less taken for granted. In the US, by contrast, powerful right-wing voices constantly question it. My debates with American libertarians have caused me to focus on issues very different from those stressed by Robert and Edward Skidelsky in their fine book.

I share Perry Anderson's concern about whether there is any hope that social science research will inspire legislative action. Having been forced to respond to libertarians' concerns in terms that might make sense to them has been an instructive exercise, one with potential to influence debate in the UK as well.

Libertarians consider it each individual's responsibility to shape his own life as he sees fit. To them, any attempt by the state to steer people toward a particular vision of the good life is unacceptable. I have therefore found it easier to engage with them by steering clear of abstract philosophical reflections about the good life and focusing instead on the many practical problems that are created by growing income inequality. It is fairly easy to demonstrate that many of the behaviours spawned by inequality are egregiously inefficient. And if you are doing something inefficiently, that implies opportunities to make everyone better off. It's easier to win agreement if the proposal is one that benefits everybody.

Libertarians acknowledge that some people are angered by the fact that others are taller, prettier or richer than they are, but insist that such hurt feelings have no legitimate place in public policy debate. But inequality isn't primarily a problem of hurt feelings.

It also gives rise to large costs that many find impossible to avoid.

To see why, it's instructive to revisit John Maynard Keynes's 1931 essay, 'Economic Possibilities for our Grandchildren'.[3] Keynes began by noting that people had two kinds of wants. Their basic needs for food and shelter had to be satisfied, but there was also a second class of wants: the desire to be seen as superior to one's neighbours, to elevate oneself above them. If productivity continued growing at its historical pace, he predicted that the first class of wants could soon be satisfied by working only a few hours a week. That prediction was basically correct.

Keynes acknowledged that wants in the second class were insatiable. But he did not think they were very important, and this point was my focus in a piece I wrote for a volume in which authors were asked to reflect on the 1931 essay.[4] Keynes has been widely described as the smartest economist of the twentieth century. How could such a man, I wondered, have believed that relative wants are unimportant?

The language he employed when speaking about relative wants provides a clue to the answer to that question. If what you are trying to do is demonstrate your superiority to your neighbours – to make them feel that you are better than they are – then that is surely a limited class of wants in society. Each of us knows people like that, to be sure, but not many of them. The phenomenon of relative wants is simply not well described as one of people wanting to demonstrate their superiority over others.

Instead, relative wants matter because our ability to achieve important goals in life depends very heavily on the context in which we try to achieve them. This way of thinking about relative wants fits the facts much more accurately than the one Keynes had in mind.

Which of the two vertical lines in Figure 1.1 is longer? You are all smart enough to suspect that it is a trick, so you may have an impulse to say they are the same. But ask yourselves this: do you think they really LOOK the same? If so, then you should consult with your neurologist, because there is probably something amiss in your brain.

To the normal human brain, the line on the right looks longer. That is just because it sits in a different context than the other one. If you think the line on the right looks longer, you are normal. There is no need to apologise.

Context shapes every evaluation that we've ever been known to make. Fresh out of college, I served as a Peace Corps volunteer in rural Nepal for two years. There, I lived in a house with two rooms, no electricity, and no running water. Never for a moment did I experience that house as unsatisfactory in any way. I was pleased to entertain my fellow teachers from the high school where I taught. I did not have children then, but if I did, they would not have been ashamed to have friends over.

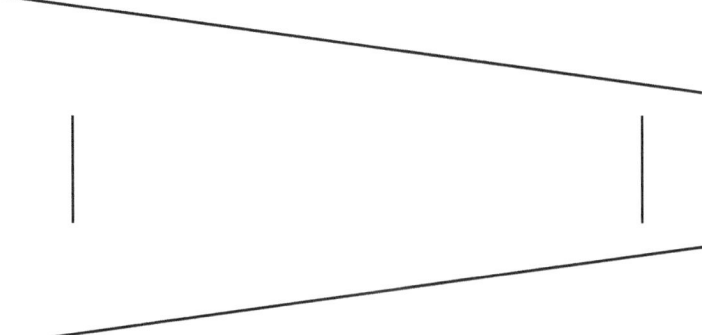

Figure 1.1 The Müller–Lyon illusion

But now I live in Ithaca, New York, where I would view that same house as totally unsatisfactory. This does not mean there is anything wrong with me. Adam Smith noted that in ancient times even the wealthiest Greeks and Romans did not feel deprived for not having a linen shirt, for such shirts did not even exist then. But in mid-18th-century Europe, he wrote, 'a creditable day-labourer would be ashamed to appear in public without a linen shirt, the want of which would be supposed to denote that disgraceful degree of poverty, which, it is presumed, nobody can well fall into without extreme bad conduct'.

If my friends from Nepal saw my current house in Ithaca, they would think that I had taken complete leave of my senses, wondering why anyone might need such a grand house. But my friends in Ithaca see it as just an ordinary professor's house, which is precisely what it is in that context.

These concerns about context seem to be hardwired. They are not something that we teach children. I did a three-day experiment with my two older sons when they were small. On day one, I gave them each a full glass of orange juice. David, aged seven, and Jason, aged five, drank without commentary. On day two, I gave each half a glass, and again they drank without commentary. There was not a whisper of complaint about their diminished portions.

On day three, I gave David a little bit more than Jason. Both glasses were nearly full and the difference between them was barely perceptible. Jason looked back and forth between them, gradually becoming more certain that the levels were different. Seeming to sense that this was not going to play out well for him, he struggled to remain silent. But finally he could contain himself no longer: 'That's not fair!' he shouted, 'he ALWAYS gets more than me!'

That was, of course, my cue to give the standard speech: 'Pay attention to your own business. If you want more orange juice, there is more in the fridge. I will get you some, ask for it politely, blah blah blah'

Most parents I know teach their children not to fret excessively about others who have nicer things. People who are inclined to do that are destined to be miserable, we tell them. There are always people out there with much more than you, and your best bet is to focus on your own business.

But would parents really want their children to be completely insensitive to the 'how am I doing?' question? The only way to answer that question is to have a frame of reference within which to think about it, and that always involves the comparison of 'how am I doing relative to people like me?'.

The most important comparisons are always local. H.L. Mencken wrote that 'a wealthy man is one who earns $200 a year more than his wife's sister's husband', so siblings seem to matter. I asked the authors of the study I am about to describe whether they were inspired by Mencken's definition. They said they had never heard of it, even though their study helps demonstrate its validity. They examined records for 3,000 pairs of full sisters, one of whom in each pair – call her Sister B – did not work outside the home. They attempted to discover which factors might predict whether her sister – Sister A – would seek paid employment. They rounded up all the usual suspects – the employment rate, her human capital measures, the vacancy rate for the area, the wage rate – none of which had any significant predictive power. Only one variable really mattered: if Sister B's husband earned more than Sister A's husband, then Sister A was 16–25 per cent more likely to seek paid employment. That does not mean she is a bad person, or that she is jealous or grasping. It means simply that context matters for evaluation. You would not want your children not to ask 'How am I doing?'. And the only way to think intelligently about that question is within a suitably chosen frame of reference.

Context matters for ordinary quality judgements. I will tell you a story about a conversation I had with Richard Posner before I gave a lecture at the University of Chicago Law School years ago. As many of you know, he is a distinguished pioneer in the law and economics movement and has been for many years a judge in the Second Circuit court in Chicago. We met for dinner the night before my talk. He drove up a little later than the appointed hour and gave his keys to the valet, who went to park it. It was a brand new Lexus sedan. As we were walking to our table, he said to me, unbidden, 'I do not know or care what kinds of cars my neighbours and colleagues drive.' He wanted me to know that.

He knew that I was going to be talking about demonstration effects in consumption and was concerned, apparently, that I might think he had bought a Lexus to impress his neighbours and colleagues. I had known Posner for 30 years and found it totally credible that he would have no idea what kinds of cars his associates drove.

I asked him why he'd bought the Lexus instead of the equally reliable Toyota by the same manufacturer. 'It is the quality of the car,' he replied. He emphasised the sound that the doors make when you close them; the smooth, buttery-soft leather on the seats; and he repeatedly mentioned one particular feature, which was the red-letter warnings in the owner's manual that you should not try to start the car up if it is already running. The engine on the Lexus is so quiet and vibration-free that this is apparently a real risk for the Lexus owner.

Most people would think ill of Posner if he had bought the Lexus to impress his neighbours and colleagues. But nobody would think ill of him for being a discerning buyer. On the contrary, we respect discerning buyers.

I asked him what car he had been driving before the Lexus. I think he said he had a five-year-old Saab. I then asked what would people think of that Saab if we could pack it up in a time capsule and send it back to 1931. He quickly responded that they would be just as impressed by it as he was by the Lexus. The car's handling, acceleration, braking and the sound of its door closing – all of that would be amazing to them. He recognised that.

There were four of us at the dinner table. I asked the others to speculate about what a formal mathematical model of the demand for quality might look like. We all agreed that we'd start by collecting data on the various characteristics of a car and compare them with the corresponding averages for other cars in the same time and place. Econometricians would estimate weights for each feature, and we'd then aggregate them into a quality index. A positive deviation for any feature would add to the quality index and a negative measure would subtract from it. We all agreed that the bigger value taken by that index, the more buyers would be willing to pay. I then pointed out that that is the same formal model we would use if we were trying to predict what a buyer would do if his goal were to demonstrate his superiority to his neighbour.

The relative wants that Keynes discussed are really not about demonstrating your superiority to others. Rather, they reflect the simple link between context and evaluation. When context matters, relative income matters. The things you have seem shabby when they are palpably worse than the things that everybody else has.

The poor in the United States are doing reasonably well in absolute terms, but what they have often seems shabby in their eyes – quite understandably, because the frame of reference is different there. If they live in a house like the one I lived in in Nepal, they would not be bad people for feeling uneasy about that.

Another important problem experienced by those with low relative income is that certain goods are available in only limited supply. Fred Hirsch, the late British economist, was a pioneer in thinking about this class of goods. He called them 'positional goods'. Everybody wants to send his children to a good school; but what is a good school? It is one that is better than the other schools in the area. If you want to send your children to a good school, you must outbid others for a house in a neighbourhood served by such a school. In virtually every country, the good schools are located in more expensive neighbourhoods. This is true even when the school budgets are, by statute, the same everywhere.

One reason is that the good schools have better students in them, in part because the children of the wealthy have more advantages. But if you are the median earner and you want to send your children to a school of just average quality, you must outbid 50 per cent of the others in the population with the same goal. Otherwise, your children will end up in schools where the students score in the twentieth percentile in reading and maths, or have metal detectors at the front entrance. Yet when all bid more vigorously for houses in better school catchment areas, they succeed only in bidding up the prices of houses in those areas. As in the familiar stadium metaphor, all stand to get a better view, but no one sees better than if all had remained comfortably seated.

There are all sorts of things we do in order to advance our interests that are, in effect, self-defeating. I mentioned that inequality is inefficient. What can parents do to help their children get ahead? One strategy might be to hold their kindergarteners back a year. The norm in the US is to start when you are five. If someone holds his child back a year – starting in kindergarten at six rather than five – he will be older, smarter, bigger, stronger and more socially skilled than his classmates. And since schools grade on a curve, he will do better each year from then on and will be more likely to get into Oxford, Harvard or Stanford, and more likely, therefore, to be successful in the job market.

But if all parents adopt that strategy, we have six-year-old kindergarteners, then seven-year-old kindergarteners, and yet no one gains relative advantage. At some point society steps in, and most jurisdictions now have mandatory kindergarten start dates. If your child turns six by 1 December of this year in Ithaca, for example, he has to start this year.

Such rules are attractive not because people are stupid, insatiable, venal or trying to show others up. They are attractive simply because relative advantage determines who gets what. Nor do such rules bespeak a nanny state imposing its vision of the good life upon us. They are a means of preventing ourselves from doing things that would be in our individual interest to do, yet are collectively bad for us. This is the essential distinction I make between the arguments I am offering and the other arguments for limiting inequality.

Almost every country now has laws against polygamy, laws that are enacted by legislatures consisting mostly of men. Many men seem to think polygamy would be a good thing because then they'd get to have several wives. But it is mathematically impossible for every male to have multiple wives. In the societies that permit polygamy, a handful of men have many wives, and many other men have none. That particular asymmetry produces a laundry list of social ills that most societies have now seen fit to avoid by trying to implement some version of monogamy statutes.

A similar logic applies to zoning laws. Business owners do not build garish, outsized signs because they are stupid. They do so to notify motorists that their businesses have something on offer, realising that signs go unnoticed unless they are bigger and brighter and stand out more than the surrounding signs. When businesses respond rationally to these incentives, we get a visual cacophony that nobody finds pleasing. The idea of having zoning laws to limit sign dimensions does not strike most reasonable people as a radical idea.

Richard Layard wrote more than 30 years ago that 'in a poor country, a man proves to his wife that he loves her by giving her a rose. In a rich country, he must give a dozen roses'. Everybody understands Layard's point. To say that context affects demand should be completely uncontroversial.

In the US, the average wedding now costs almost $30,000. In 1980, it was $11,000. Nobody thinks that people getting married today are happier because they are spending so much more. Rather, there has been an expenditure cascade that has shifted the standard that defines adequacy.

Virtually all of the income growth during the last four decades has gone to the top of the income ladder. The middle class does not get jealous when they see the mansions and yachts purchased by the rich. Indeed, they seem to enjoy seeing pictures of them. But higher spending at the top shifts the frame of reference that defines what the people just below them feel they need. Their daughters need to get married at home now, instead of in a hotel, so they too build bigger, and so on all the way down the income ladder.

The median new house built in the US was 2,300 square feet in 2007, more than 50 per cent larger than its counterpart in 1970, even though the median earner did not have more purchasing power in real terms. The hourly wage in real terms is actually lower than it was then. The median earners are spending more on housing because others like them are spending more, and if they do not match what others are spending, they will have to send their children to bad schools.

The resulting spending patterns are grossly inefficient. The rich do not have an interest in having to spend $10 million for their daughter's coming-of-age party, as one CEO did in New York recently. But if that is what people like you are spending, then that is what you spend, rather than risk disappointing people you care so much about.

Is there anything to be done? On this question, the Skidelskys and I arrive at the same spot in the end. I have been proposing a progressive tax on consumption for more than 30 years now and am delighted to see them embrace this proposal. The basic idea is simple. You report your income to the tax authorities as you do now, and you also report how much you saved during the year – as we already do for tax-free retirement accounts. Your income minus your savings is how much you spent during the year, and that amount minus a big standard deduction (to allow for the people at the bottom who do not save much) is your taxable consumption. Taxes are levied on that amount, with rates that start very low, then rise steadily as taxable consumption rises.

That simple policy change would deflect much of today's luxury consumption into additional investment. Having more investment and fewer mansions and expensive parties will help fuel additional growth. Growth in certain kinds of consumption threatens the environment, and we need to use available policy levers – such as a tax on carbon emissions – to restrain growth in those areas. But when income grows, a lot of aspects of society that we really value get better. The air gets cleaner, the cures for diseases are discovered more quickly, and so on.

Many people applaud a progressive consumption tax in principle only to lament that its adoption would be politically impossible. But although tax policy changes are always difficult, support for the progressive consumption tax is surprisingly diverse. A progressive consumption tax was proposed in the US Senate during 1995, for example, under bipartisan sponsorship.

One week after I published an article about this tax in 1997, I received a warm letter from Milton Friedman, who began by saying that he didn't agree with me that the US government should be raising and spending additional revenue (federal budgets at the time were edging toward surplus). But he quickly went on to add that if the government did need additional revenue, a progressive consumption tax would be by far the best way to raise it. He enclosed a reprint of his 1943 American Economic Review article in which he advocated a progressive consumption tax as the best way to pay for World War II. More recently, two economists from the American Enterprise Institute, a conservative think tank, have published a book extolling the virtues of a progressive consumption tax.

This tax would not only promote the vision of the good life described by the Skidelskys in *How Much Is Enough?*, it would also help eliminate much of the waste inherent in current spending patterns.

Discussion

Richard Seaford
Robert Skidelsky seemed to be saying that there is a natural human insatiability which money caters for, whereas goods do not, or do not to the same extent.

I am wondering whether that is lethally the wrong model, and whether it has negative political consequences. What one should do here is to look at pre-monetary societies; and, if there are no pre-monetary societies left, to look at our records of pre-monetary societies. We should ask whether human insatiability is part of those societies.

The pre-monetary society that I know best is Homer's. Now, if you look at Homeric society, you do not find insatiability as a part of human nature. In the 5th century BC there is an obsession with the dangers of unlimited desire, expressed in accumulation of money. In Homer, there is no such concern, because there is no such insatiability. The point that I am making here is that you must not posit a human nature and suppose that different social formations allow it more or less scope. We must suppose that it is the social formation that creates what we imagine to be human nature, which differs according to different formations.

There are two reasons, in a pre-monetary society, why unlimited desire really has no place. One is that, to reiterate a point Robert Skidelsky made, there is no point having 20 million tripods. The other is the social code which limits the unlimited desire for goods, or does not allow it to emerge. For example, the status which comes from giving – if you are wealthy, you give, and that is how you create a following – has within it a mechanism that is always going to limit the amount that you possess individually. Agamemnon has a concern for status, and so does Achilles, but Agamemnon has to give, and the Iliad is about that process breaking down.

Now, what money does when it is invented – in my view – towards the end of the 6th century BC is to allow for the first time in history a code of acquisitive individualism that is still with us. There are practical reasons why money, being concealable, transportable, storable, and so on, lends itself to individual ownership in a way that no pre-monetary good does. That creates the illusion of self-sufficiency and marginalises the social duty to give. You can see that whole process of individualism, and in particular acquisitive individualism, coming into being by looking at ancient Greek texts. You can actually see it before your very eyes, and the big mistake politically for our purposes is to imagine that human insatiability is part of human nature.

Robert Skidelsky
May I ask Richard a question? Did the whole of economics start on the wrong basis, with Adam Smith's 'inborn desire for improvement'? And then Scitovsky comes in with a much later version of insatiability for novelty, because we get bored with what we have. Is that all wrong? Economists will attribute that to human nature, but you are saying it is actually the result of the particular society in which you live.

Richard Seaford
Yes, I am. David Graeber, who is an anthropologist, will know much more about this than I do, but my immediate response to your question is that the economic approach is completely wrong, because it is not true of all societies.

Felix Martin
It is all very well to say, 'traditional society had many different axes and scales of worth with which people could evaluate actions and their place in society, whereas in modern, monetary society we have the single, imperialistic concept of universal economic value'. But the point is that monetary society allows us to be dynamic. These traditional societies were essentially static. It is the dynamism that allows all these relative comparisons. The point is that in traditional society it was meaningless to say, 'I am a peasant, but I would like to become the king'.

It does not make any sense whatsoever. That only makes sense with the technology of money.

I want to make this point, because it is important that we should not be totally negative about money and monetary society. There is a lot of negative stuff about money, but this aspect of dynamism is what is good about it. It is all very well to say that in traditional societies people had other ways of feeling good about themselves, but the truth is that, for most people, it just meant that they had many other ways of feeling bad about themselves. It is not that there were other ways to advance themselves; it is that there was no way for them to advance themselves.

John Milbank
I wanted to ask Perry Anderson a question. I totally agree with him that agency is the crucial issue, but I wondered whether implicit in what you are saying is a certain duality between ideals on the one hand and agency – regarded as a kind of material force – on the other. I think this model looks doubtful, because you seem to be asking, 'where is the next distress going to come from that will automatically produce the agency that will cause change?'. I think the contrast between now and the 19th and early 20th centuries is that we have tons of distress, but we do not have agency. In other words, agency does not happen automatically in response to distress.

All the early labour movements were moved by either religion – and there were more Catholics than Marxists – or else by secular equivalents of religion. They believed in agency because they had an ontology that had a place for agency, whether it was Marxist or religious. The problem now is that we are all so sucked into systems that most people do not think of themselves as agents any longer. That is the real issue. The problem is not where agency will come from, but how to reinvent agency. Agency is not something simply material, and on this point, religious people – even if they are in an increasing minority – are much more likely to believe in agency than other people. That is why it is possible that religious people will play a disproportionate role in relation to their numbers in the future, and I think that that is already happening.

Perry Anderson
That is a very interesting observation, and certainly it is true that simple distress or disaster in itself does not generate agencies of change. It is a condition of such change. On the other hand, I do think that you have to look at identifiable social groups in the society today if you are to have any kind of sense of how things might change. You need both. You need the ideas, and the programmes that go together with ideas, as well as the actual social forces.

Robert Skidelsky
Could I just ask Bob Frank about this? He has been, as he said, advocating a progressive consumption tax for 30 years, and it has not happened. Where is your agency, apart from your own eloquence?

Robert H. Frank
One thing I have come to believe more and more as I have thought about this is that it is very difficult to predict where ideas are going to go. If you have been following the same-sex marriage issue as it has evolved in the US in the press, there was a very big majority adamantly opposed to any idea of allowing same-sex marriage as recently as ten years ago. There was a majority as recently as two or three years ago. In another two years, 75 per cent of the American public will think, 'what is the problem with same-sex marriage? Why did

we think before that we should not have allowed that?'. A lot of what seems okay to think about doing depends on what other people think is okay to think about doing, and there are such rich network interdependencies in 'who thinks what about what' that it is very difficult to predict how opinion about an issue will evolve.

Nobody feels now that we do not need to raise money. There are a few eccentrics who argue that we can just cut wasteful government spending, but nobody who has looked at the numbers thinks that we do not need to raise money. There are now two conservative economists at the American Enterprise Institute who have a new book out advocating a progressive consumption tax.[5] I am not sure we need a new concept of agency; we need a bill in the Senate. We had one in 1996. Sam Nunn and Pete Domenici – Democrat and Republican – proposed a progressive consumption tax. It never came up for a vote, because other things crowded it off the table, but it was not seen as highly controversial. It is a win–win move. Conservative businessmen do not have any interest in having to build 60,000 square feet just because others like them have mansions that big and that is what you need to be able to entertain in the style that everybody expects. It would be much better to have 20,000 square feet if everybody else did. We know that if there was 100 per cent tax on spending beyond $4 million a year, then people would build small. There really is some easy stuff to do if you could get the conversation going.

Perry Anderson
If I might just quickly rejoin, the transformation in opinions regarding same-sex marriage is very striking, but there is no material cost involved whatsoever. It is no skin off anybody's economic nose, but with the

expenditure tax, you really have to ask yourself, 'if it is as obvious and as rational as that, how on earth is it that 30 years have gone by and it has never been implemented?'. There has to be more than 'people were distracted, or not paying attention'.

Robert H. Frank
I will go one better. There is not only no cost to implementing a progressive consumption tax, but there are – by my back-of-the-envelope calculations – $2 trillion in benefits from adopting one.

Perry Anderson
But then my question becomes even stronger. Why on earth has it not happened?

Robert H. Frank
That is a fair question: 'If I am so smart, why am I not rich?' The fact is that many policies could be implemented that would make the overall pie bigger but would injure specific people, and they are not implemented because those people scream so loudly that they are effectively able to block it. I think that is a failure of the policy-maker's imagination in not coming up with ways to compensate the losers. If the pie is bigger, there is enough there to compensate the losers. If you have people who are in a position to block a move that would make the pie bigger, they have got you, and they can demand compensation. Why not pay them? If the mansion-builders need compensation, give them a payment.

Robert Skidelsky
So why have we not had a progressive consumption tax, despite all the practical and theoretical arguments in its favour? The reason is that people do not think that consumption is bad. They may have real objections to highly unequal incomes which they do not have to

highly unequal consumption. I do not know why – one can explore that – but the reason one has not had the progressive consumption tax is because there is much less objection to consumption than to income.

What that suggests to me is that Bob cannot evade the question of the ends of economic activity. You made a very plausible case for trying to get the low-lying fruit and postponing any higher order discussion, since we can deal with these easy things fairly easily. However, it turns out that you cannot deal with the easy things because they are not adopting your ideas. Therefore, you actually have to get into the higher order things, and that brings one to the subject of our book, which is 'what are the ends of life? What is the process for?'.

Robert H. Frank
However, we have the same policy proposal. In my context, I do not think I would be more likely to succeed in getting people to consider it if I offered an ethical critique of money than if I pointed out to people how they would be happier paying higher taxes and driving a slightly less expensive car. Let's say the choice is between a Porsche 911 and a Ferrari 456. If you can drive the cheaper car on a well-paved road, would you be happier than if you drove the more expensive one on roads riddled with potholes?

Phillip Blond
My point would be that you would be far more likely to get your consumption tax if you did a first order move, because a proper politics creates the audience it wants to speak to. Because moral activity – to go back to the Greeks – is about who you ought to be, it is that 'ought', which Robert and Edward's book speaks to, that matters. People can be politically converted to that 'ought'. It seems to me that agency is not material. It is ideal.

Robert H. Frank
To Robert, I would say that it is an ethical critique that I offer, albeit a consequentialist one. I do not think you should restrict anyone, unless it is to prevent him from harming others. If I spend $10 million on my child's birthday party, I harm others by shifting the frame of reference that defines what constitutes an adequate celebration of a special occasion. Middle-class families now have to hire a clown or a magician for their kids' birthday parties. They did not have to do that.

Perry Anderson
On the question of changes of value, the simple point I wanted to make this morning is that the proposals which you find in Robert and Edward's book are not very radical ones. However, it is not plausible to me that they could be realised without changes of real magnitude, either at the level of social actors or at the level of economic or ecological shocks – or, indeed, for those who think this is plausible, some really new religious awakening. Small, incremental changes of the kind that are the stuff of everyday politics today do not in any way match the magnitude of what is envisaged.

Phillip Blond
Bob Frank says that comparisons are local and relational, but what has happened in the modern world, via advertising and globalisation, is that our comparator has centralised. We have lost any ability to develop indigenous local evaluation or an indigenous way of feeling good about ourselves and what we do. We now compare ourselves to people who are out of our group as if they were in our group, and this is incredibly socially destructive. It drains the local person who runs the football team or who does good by his or her neighbours of any value, and I think that is the crucial structural shift.

Robert H. Frank
I am familiar with the thesis that it is the fact that we can see people in distant places that has shifted our frame of reference. I am not sympathetic to that thesis. I think we could always see people with much more than we have, even locally – unless we were right at the top locally – and, again, the people in the middle do not seem discomforted by the fact that others who are way above them have so much more. That does not seem to be a source of distress for people. The comparisons that matter in the university are with people in the same group you are in, not with people in the building across the courtyard. The comparisons people make are still very local.

Phillip Blond
If that was true, there would not be advertising.

Robert H. Frank
Advertising affects us, of course. It puts ideas of what would be fun to have into our heads. Those messages have an effect, but they have always had an effect. We have always seen pictures of nice things and known there were nice things out there that we could not have, so that is not a new thing. What has changed is the pattern of income growth, and in particular the spectacular incomes earned at the top of every group. That pattern is completely fractal. It is local: if you look at real estate agents, you see the same pattern there. The ones in the middle have the same income as 30 years ago and the ones at the top are doing spectacularly better. It is true for dentists. It is the same pattern in virtually every occupation you can name. It is the same in each state and each city.

The comparisons that matter are not with people way above you, but people like you. 'What is the right house for people like me?' The answer to that question has changed because of the change in purchasing power. I do not believe it is to do with anything we see on the TV. I think we can change that situation. You cannot change the market forces that are concentrating income at the top – or at least, I do not see any way to eliminate the technological changes that have fuelled that movement – but you can change the distribution of after-tax expenditures that people make. I think that is what is driving the expenditure cascades that have made achieving ordinary goals more difficult for people in the middle.

Richard Bronk

I agree with Robert Frank about positional goods. It seems to me that this is really the key element of insatiability that is missing in economic models. It is usually seen in terms of status, but it is not status. Positional goods are a fixed supply, like houses in Manhattan or houses in London. In crowded countries, in crowded cities, goods that we like for their intrinsic value can become congested. They either get rationed by higher prices or congested, so we have defensive spending, and so relative wealth becomes key again. Then you are back to the fixed cake problem. I have a little quote from Fred Hirsch, who wrote about this at length: 'Rather than trinkets, the distinctive appurtenances of the rich then become squirrels' wheels for those below: objects of desire that the most intensive effort cannot reach'.[6] That was his comment.

Notes

1. James Buchan, *Frozen Desire: An Inquiry into the Meaning of Money* (London: Picador, 1998).
2. John Maynard Keynes, *Essays in Persuasion*, in *The Collected Writings of John Maynard Keynes*, vol. 9 (Cambridge: Cambridge University Press, 1978), p. 293.
3. Ibid.

4. Lorenzo Pecchi and Gustavo Piga (eds), *Revisiting Keynes* (Cambridge, MA: MIT Press, 2010).
5. Alan D. Viard and Robert Carroll, *Progressive Consumption Tax: The X-Tax Revisited* (Washington, DC: AEI Press, 2012).
6. Fred Hirsch, *Social Limits to Growth* (London: Routledge, 1977), p. 66.

Session 2

Equality and Corruption

Steven Lukes

The question I have in mind relates to the general title we have been given of 'Markets and Morals'. The question is: what exactly are the harms that markets do? By 'markets' I mean buying and selling goods and services.

I am not going to deal with the good things that markets do. Market exchange brings about dynamism, the capacity for innovation, the acquisition of knowledge and the communication of information that is unavailable by any other means, the enhancement of choice, success in promoting long-term economic growth, the securing of liberty for whole segments of the population that were excluded by hierarchies of various kinds and the introduction of certain kinds of equality. All of these things we know about.

I will instead focus on the question of what is wrong with markets. This is a fundamental question asked at a certain level of abstraction, like the question 'how much is enough?'. I want to approach it in that spirit.

Two books have just come out with very similar titles and, curiously enough, neither of them refers to the other. One is by a former student of mine, Michael Sandel, called *What Money Can't Buy*. The other one is by philosopher Debra Satz and is called *Why Some Things Should Not Be For Sale*.[1] They are about exactly these questions:

Equality and Corruption 45

where do markets invade? Where is market exchange inappropriate?

I am not going to talk about the policy question – 'what to do about it?' – which is dealt with by Robert Frank, Robert Skidelsky and Perry Anderson. It may well be that we decide that markets cause harms that are unavoidable, that there may be no institutional alternative or maybe the only way to deal with the harms that a market causes is to introduce another kind of market, as in carbon trading, for example.

I think we need a distinction between what you might call intrinsic harms – that is, harms that are held to occur under all conceivable circumstances, even the most favourable – and what you might call aggravating harms – that is to say, harms that occur in the feasible world – in the world that is recognisably sufficiently like our own to be regarded as realistic. The facts about actual markets become very important when looking at harm in that second sense. In order to look at intrinsic harms we have to engage in what Margaret Radin, who wrote a book called *Contested Commodities*[2] calls with some scepticism 'professors' hypotheticals', where you are supposed to imagine alternative worlds.

There are two broad arguments here. The first is the argument that markets corrupt. I think this argument is about intrinsic harm: the harm of commodification. Then there is a different kind of argument, which has to do with equality (see Glen Newey below in this session). However, I do think they come together.

First of all, let us look at the argument that markets corrupt. That is a very old story, of course. It goes all the way back to the money changers in the temple and medieval arguments about usury. It really set in as a serious discussion in the 19th century, with the most classic and famous sentence in this literature coming from

The Communist Manifesto, where Marx and Engels write about the role of naked self-interest, with human relations becoming drowned in the 'icy water of egotistical calculation'. That is the English translation of a text to rival the King James Bible; it is a wonderful phrase.

To be precise about this: what do we mean by commodification? What are we talking about here? I want to quote a very helpful account of commodification, an analysis of what its component features are, which comes from Margaret Radin's book. She says there are four features of commodification. They are:

- *Objectification*. That is to say, treating persons and things instrumentally, as manipulable at will.
- *Fungibility*. That is, where the goods in question are fully interchangeable with no effect on their value to the holder.
- *Commensurability*, which is where their values can be arrayed as a function of one continuous variable or can be linearly ranked.
- Fourth – and often this is the most important – *money-equivalence*, where the continuous variable in terms of which they can be ranked is monetary value.

This argument – and you find this certainly in the Marx and Engels' version of this – splits into two features, namely what you might call corruption and contamination. That is to say, goods and services are commodified and they are said to be debased or distorted by being commodified, i.e. treated as marketable. Then the idea is that the infection and contamination spreads across persons and goods, so that the corruption extends to other goods and services and it becomes a generalised phenomenon.

Sandel's book is the most recent and certainly very eloquent and powerfully expressed statement of this case.

Equality and Corruption

The main thing about the book is that it is full of examples. The examples are intended to support the claim of corruption. He writes, 'to corrupt a good or a social practice is to degrade it' – 'to treat it according to a lower mode of valuation than is appropriate to it'. He also writes that 'implicit in any charge of corruption is a conception of the purposes and ends that an institution properly pursues' and that we 'corrupt a good, an activity or a social practice when we treat it according to a lower norm than is appropriate to it'. So the key question to ask is: what is the meaning of the good in question? We see that markets and commerce change the character of a good they touch and when we see this we have to ask where markets belong and where they do not. We cannot answer this question without deliberating about the meaning and purpose of goods and the values that should govern them.

For example, Sandel argues, 'friendship and the social practices that sustain it are constituted by certain norms, attitudes and values. Commodifying these practices displaces these norms – sympathy, generosity, thoughtfulness, attentiveness – and replaces them with market values'. The book proceeds through a series of case studies of corruption, and among the examples marshalled to illustrate this general claim are:

- ways of jumping the queue such as afforded by ticket scalpers and concierge doctors;
- paying cash for sterilisation;
- bribing kids for good grades and adults to lose weight;
- selling the right to immigrate;
- trading procreation permits or pollution permits or carbon offsets;
- paying to kill an endangered rhino;
- auctioning college admissions;
- selling blood;

- markets in life and death, such as so-called 'janitor's insurance', where employers take out life insurance policies on their own employees;
- internet death pools;
- the terrorism futures market;
- skyboxes at baseball games;
- commercials in the classroom.

I am not sure I feel equally badly about all of these, but it is an interesting and impressive list of allegedly corrupt practices. I am not convinced that there is a unified account that you could give about what is wrong with these. They seem to me to be of significantly different weight. However, they are all examples of something interesting. Although these books do not refer to each other, Debra Satz, who writes about equality and inequality, does have a view about this argument, which she rejects. She says that there are rival views of the meaning of many particular goods and of human flourishing and, more importantly, that there is only a tenuous connection in most cases between the meaning we give to a good and its distribution by a market. It is often quite unclear whether buying and selling damages such goods and, if so, how. That seems to me to be undoubtedly true.

The fact that these meanings are contested and often unclear does not mean that there is not something deeply and important to consider. I would like to refer here to an interesting sociologist called Viviana Zelizer, who has written about the link between intimacy and commercial activity.[3] Her work is about the way in which the exchange of money and intense interest in money and payments is deeply involved in all kinds of relationships, both at the level of everyday life in, for example, relationships between intimates in marriages and so on, but also in court cases where issues arise about who owes what to whom. In other words, her basic line is that we should relax about all of this and recognise that commercial transactions are just part of everyday life in ways which we often do not even think about. The idea that there are what she calls 'hostile worlds' – that there is the world of money exchange and the world of friendship and intimacy and valued relationships, which are separate spheres and hostile to one another – is a kind of fiction. In fact, they are far more intimately related than that argument would suggest. In its place, she proposes what she calls the perspective of 'connected lives'.

Going back to Margaret Radin's fourfold distinction and the different components of commodification, just take, for example, the first one. Is treating persons and things instrumentally a problem? I would raise the following objection. Are there not many contexts, especially in modern urban living, in which instrumental relationships – seeing the world in anonymous and commensurable terms and, indeed, often in monetary ways – are much to be valued? Indeed, are instrumental relationships not sometimes the essential precondition for and counterpoint to mutual relationships in more intimate settings?

You want your doctor to have a bedside manner, but you also want patients to have hospital numbers and medical resources to be rationally allocated on objective grounds, whatever these may be. This should always be done with discretion. I remember once being in hospital with an Achilles tendon, when the doctors congregated in the corner to discuss how old I was. That was not a very pleasant experience, but nevertheless one wants these decisions to be made and rationally made.

It is not even obvious that treating people as objects and as a means to some end is always a bad idea. It surely must depend on the end and on who is doing what in pursuing it. According to his biographer, Beethoven was 'filled with a deep conviction as to the significance of his work and his art'. In 1801, he referred to two of his friends as 'merely instruments on which to play when I feel inclined. I value them merely for what they do for me'. As for commensurability and incommensurability, why should we assume that we cannot both know the price of something and know that it is priceless? Indeed, Zelizer wrote a book called *Pricing the Priceless Child*. Do we not make insurance decisions, and pay medical administrators and policymakers to allocate resources and plan the siting of airports on the basis that alternative options involve injury or death? Of course, this is statistical death: in other words, the statistical probability of deaths and injuries that we expect to be costed on a rational and systematic basis, a basis that puts a regularly updated and commercially based value on human life. The American agency called OSHA every six months publishes a value placed upon life, and that is a precondition for public policy-making. Interestingly, this value is not widely discussed. The *routes nationales* in France have beautiful trees that are aligned along the sides of the roads, which are responsible for a certain number of statistically predictable deaths every year, but the trees remain.

What is clear is that we do make these choices, and we live with them. But it is also clear that sometimes when goods or services are monetised something is going wrong and we should be disturbed about it. Sometimes it is fairly obvious that corruption is taking place. One example of this – though nothing is straightforward here – is so-called 'Baumol goods'. This term comes from the economist William Baumol, who argued that services that resist commodification are those where the human touch is crucial and are more resistant to labour productivity growth. They resist standardisation because treatment must be tailored to the individual case and quality is – or at least is believed to be – inescapably correlated with the amount of human labour devoted to their production. His original example was the performing arts, but then this analysis was extended to other services including teaching, doctoring and policing.

Here it becomes complicated. You could say that Baumol underestimated the way in which things have gone in our societies. Capital displays a constant resourcefulness in its efforts to resolve the problems it confronts, including the ability to wean consumers from services into consuming material goods, providing the labour component themselves, and finally consigning any residue to small high-end markets or leaving them to increasingly beleaguered state provision. You might ask what exactly is objectionable here. In Britain, for instance, the commodification of medical services has involved the splitting up of different services, not all of which are Baumol-like in resisting productivity increments, while enlisting patients in the provision of the service is not always a bad idea. On the other hand, I can report that in America, unless you are lucky, your doctor is going to give you very little time and it is all increasingly marketdriven. Not only is there increasing consumption of drugs and painkillers, but speeding up of the examination of patients is widespread.

I am really making the point that there are some goods for which marketisation changes their nature and, although there is room for dispute, the range of such dispute is limited. I think one area where you could say that the nature of a good is imperilled by marketisation is what we might call the conditions of citizenship and, in particular, the conditions of good citizenship. Here, I am thinking particularly of education and public broadcasting, which of course in the age of the internet is becoming more and more important. However, again reporting my experience of America, I yearn for the BBC. In America, the provision of information in a trustable and reliable way is now restricted to something that is called public broadcasting but in fact is largely supported by and confined to a very small segment of viewers and listeners.

One general argument about corruption comes from Karl Polanyi, who argued in his book *The Great Transformation*[4] that the disembedding of the economy in the course of the great transformation was destructive. In the course of the building of a self-regulating market economy, the three factors of production – labour, land and money – came to be treated as ordinary commodities and subject to market exchange. Although there are many things you could say in criticism of Polanyi and, in particular, his doom-laden view about the future of capitalism, the book has a renewed relevance today.

The idea of fictitious commodities – his key example was money – is the centrepiece of his argument. His idea was that what he calls 'fictitious commodification' is the attempt to commodify the market's very conditions of possibility. One interpretation of what he is saying is that labour, land and money are constitutive of the very fabric of social life; they form the necessary background for commodity production and exchange. What he is getting at is that you cannot have commodification that goes all the way down. As he wrote, 'to allow the market mechanism to be the sole director of the fate of human beings in their natural environment would result in the demolition of society'. That is a general argument about the way in which commodification can destroy. In a sense, you could say, paradoxically, what we are seeing is the reverse process, in which social relationships are increasingly embedded in the market itself.

Equality and Corruption

Let me turn now to the inequality argument, which is developed in the book by Debra Satz. She sets out to ask the questions, 'which markets are noxious? Which markets are doing harm?'. Her central concern is not with corruption but with inequality. By 'equality' she means – and this is where citizenship comes in – the idea of a society where everyone has equal standing, equal status. She proposes that harmful markets, noxious markets, are those which undermine the conditions that people need if they are to relate as equals – as individuals with equal standing. She illustrates this thought with a rather wonderful little parable from Thomas Schelling, namely the case of the sinking *Titanic*, in which there were only enough lifeboats for first class and the steerage was expected to go down with the ship. Schelling wrote, 'we no longer tolerate this. If some people cannot afford the price of passage with lifeboats and some people can, they should not be travelling on the same ship.'

Her general argument is that an equal society, in her sense, can be undermined in two main ways: either a given market can produce extremely harmful outcomes for individuals or for society, by supporting relations of humiliating subordination or unaccountable power; or else, secondly, the underlying conditions of the market agents can be highly unequal, as when some are seriously lacking in agency or knowledge or some are significantly more vulnerable than others. The examples she takes, which are different from Sandel's, are markets in women's reproductive labour, in women's sexual labour (prostitution), in child labour, in involuntary slavery, and in organ transplants – human kidneys, in particular.

This interesting argument is not, I think, an argument about intrinsic harm. It is not an argument about the damage that the marketising of goods and services does to the good itself, but rather it is an argument in terms of what she calls 'contextual reasons'. That is to say, given the world as it is and the world as it is likely to be, the marketing is damaging and harmful to equality. The example that she gives is prostitution. She argues about prostitution that given currently prevailing beliefs and attitudes this market perpetuates status inequality between men and women. As she puts it in a graphic phrase, 'prostitution is a theatre of inequality because it displays for us a practice in which women are seen as servants of men's desires and it shapes and influences the ways in which women as a whole are seen'. Stigma surrounds the practice and is reinforced by it. In a different culture perhaps things could be otherwise, but she doubts this very seriously. She criticises feminists who argue that prostitutes can function as sex therapists fulfilling a legitimate social need, as well as providing a source of social experiment and alternative conceptions of sexuality and gender. She writes, 'such feminists have minimised the cultural stereotypes that surround contemporary prostitution and exaggerated their own power to shape the practice. Prostitution, like pornography, is not easily separated from the larger surrounding culture that marginalises, stereotypes and stigmatises women'. She says, 'I think we need to look carefully at what men and women actually learn in prostitution and I doubt that ethnographic studies of prostitution would support the claim that prostitution adds to women's dignity or empowerment'.

She argues – and this is the point about contextual reasons – that the powerful intuition here that prostitution is intrinsically degrading is bound up with well-entrenched views of male gender identity and women's sexual role in the context of that identity. Prostitution is connected to stigma, unequal status and thus to injustice, operating through beliefs and attitudes which, although theoretically they could be changed so that buying and selling sex might not involve any of those harms, she does not believe they could be in the foreseeable future.

Here you have a specific example of an argument for the harm that markets do being a harm to the prospect of an equal society, in her sense. The question is to what extent this claim can be generalised. The harm here is an aggravating harm; it is a harm that aggravates inequalities of resources, information and agency that results from those background inequalities and will survive in all feasible circumstances. The more general claim is thus the need for rights; hence the need for citizenship rights that takes us back to the whole debate about social democracy articulated most eloquently by T. H. Marshall in his *Citizenship and Social Class*,[5] which provides the most powerful case that I know of for the limitation of the market on these grounds.

Those aggravating harms are important to think about. We really rely on a perspective that is closer to the facts than we find typically in mainstream economics. Economists are very good at imagining a world in which the background conditions are such as to allow us to believe that equality of status or standing is not damaged; in other words, where markets can occur without damage to equality. Insofar as economics increasingly shapes the way in which we see the world that we live in, the danger is that we can come to conceive of the world as if it were the idealised world.

Glen Newey

Steven Lukes has dealt with corruption and equality in relation to markets. What I will do now is to pursue further that inquiry, but with respect to a specific example. I take it that there is an intuitive repugnance to some of the ways in which markets operate; Steven gave a good list from Sandel of the various morally dubious contexts in which markets can emerge. Here are a couple of further examples from recent news. There was a story last week about a man in India who tried to sell a baby via Facebook, unbeknownst to the baby's mother. That was detected and prevented, but selling the baby seemed to be the man's intention. A second case dates from a few years ago, but sentencing was delayed because of appeals from the defendant's attorneys. A judge in a Pennsylvania court was found to have struck a deal with private prison operators whereby he would give maximum-tariff custodial sentences to children accused in court, because then they could pass those on to prison operators, whose remuneration depended on the number of prison places filled. He was sending ten-year-old children off to jail for having dropped candy wrappers on the pavement and similarly trivial offences; the other day he was sentenced to 28 years. These examples are outrageous really, but as a philosopher one has to try, not to temper one's outrage necessarily, but to try to explain it or justify it – and that is where the interesting but problematic questions arise.

The example that I promised you is an unfamiliar one in the sense that it is one that has not been actively discussed in the public sphere, yet at the same time it is certainly not my invention. It is simply this: should we be able to buy and sell votes? I take that partly for its intrinsic importance and interest, but also because it is quite a good way of throwing into relief the different justifications that might be traded back and forth by people on either side of the argument. Obviously, the intrinsic outrageousness reaction comes in at this point.

As background, I take it that votes are a sort of in-kind benefaction bestowed by the state on democratic citizens in the form of the franchise: an in-kind good, like healthcare. You cannot just decide that you will waive, for example, your right to treatment on the NHS in exchange for a cash payment or similar which has in principle a certain marketable value. It is not, as things stand, something you can commodify. The supply is limited, so I am assuming that this works in the context of a system where there is one person, one vote, as in this country with national elections. Then the suggestion which has been espoused by some economists – Robert Russell was in conversation with Debra Satz about this question online and is one supporter of it[6] – is should we allow the buying and selling of votes? If not, why not?

Let me give a quick overview of the case for. One possible objection that might come up straightaway, which I am going to put to one side, is that it is literally unimaginable. We are in the realm of professors' hypotheticals again here, I guess, but as we know from the last 30 years, these suggestions which seem outlandish have a habit of working their way into the public sphere. At any rate, I do not think it is an impossible proposal. I assume that what would happen if such a proposal were implemented is that intermediaries, brokerage firms, would buy up people's votes in the same way as buying equities on the open market, for example; those assets would then have a market position. Votes would have different values depending on local psephological circumstances, for example. Those intermediary agencies, the brokerage firms, would be in a position to ask the people who stand for election – political parties, let us assume – to take a particular position in return for their votes; for instance, a position favoured by lobbies who were paying the brokerage firms to cast the vote a certain way. So the firms' immediate paymasters would be the lobbies (channelling, we may assume, funds from industry and other interests with the necessary financial muscle); but they would then be engaged in negotiation with political parties to agree a manifesto position in exchange for their votes. Those who so wished could retain their vote and exercise it as individuals do now. Maybe the market would work differently from this; but what is intended here is merely to provide an indication of how it could work, so meeting the concern about impossibility. So, as far as the imaginability goes, it seems to me there is not a problem. There are obviously different ways in which such a system could operate and I am not going to go further into the details of that.

What is the argument for such a market? The main argument is that it is a Pareto superior outcome. Obviously, some people who have a vote will want to keep their vote, because they want to exercise their democratic right, and there is nothing in this proposal that rules that out. At the same time, many people do not vote: about 50 per cent of the registered electorate in the US, for example, do not vote in national elections such as the quadrennial one to elect the president; the abstention figures are not quite that high in national elections over here, but a significant percentage stays at home nonetheless. This is increasing in secular terms. Somebody might then think this vote is useless, and might as well be sold. 'I am not going to vote. I am not interested in politics, so I will sell it at whatever the going rate is.' This is really what the underpinnings of so-called revealed preference theory are: the very fact that I undertake a trade of my vote with some brokerage agency of the sort just described means that we – that is, you and I, supposing you run the brokerage firm – both get to a better position. I have reached a better position because I have cash in exchange for my vote, which I prefer, and you, the agency, have got to a better position because it prefers having my vote to having this marginal amount of cash which it has put my way in exchange for it.

That is the Pareto case for a market in votes. I take it that is the standard argument for marketisation in particular contexts, applied to voting. What I am going to do now is run the corruption and equality objections past this proposal to see how well it stands up.

Again, taking corruption first, I think that it is a term that needs explication in Sandel and elsewhere. It is a term with a very long history, as people will be aware. There is a way of using the term 'corruption' which, it seems to me, simply restates in another form the proposition that market relations are being introduced in some area of social life where hitherto they have not been present. On this view, it is the very fact of monetisation which involves corruption. That may or may not be true, but it does not seem to have independent argumentative status, as it were. All it has done is introduce a 'boo word', as the old emotivists called it, namely 'corruption', in place of a more neutral description of what is being advocated. It does not seem to me that corruption, in that minimal sense, really gets the argument any further, so let us look at some other ways in which it might be understood.

A very important version of the idea, sometimes introduced by the notion of denaturing something, is that what is called its internal goal or internal aim is somehow stymied or frustrated by marketisation. A version of this argument comes up in Robert Nozick, with regard to the provision of medical services.[7] Before Nozick wrote his book, the philosopher Bernard Williams had argued that the internal goal of medical practice is to provide healthcare, and you get a kind of denaturing in the sense that the internal goal is frustrated if that is then distributed not on the basis of need, but on the basis of ability to pay. To that argument Nozick responds that one can imagine an alternative practice called 'schmoctoring' rather than 'doctoring', which is such that its internal goal is to earn money for the practitioner. Then you do not get the same problem about denaturing the internal goal of schmoctoring that you had with doctoring. In other words, you move the goalposts so you just create a kind of parallel activity, which is such that the cash nexus is essentialised as the internal goal of the activity. Of course, one can say that it is obvious that the goal of medicine is healthcare, and that Nozick's argument is a bit of sophistry. But it's far less clear with the vote what its internal goal might be.

So one might say perhaps it perverts the aim of the vote, which is an arguable proposition. If, for example, the aim of the vote is that the citizens en masse get the opportunity to participate in the public political life of their society, then that aim will be frustrated, at least in part. If some people are just trading their votes for cash, then one of the things that they have abrogated in so doing is their right to public political participation. However, somebody might say, 'Well, it is up for grabs democratically what the point of the democratic vote is.' What the aim or justification of the franchise is, as opposed to simply the procedural mechanisms by means of which it is affected, is something which can be further debated. Indeed, political theorists debate this amongst themselves, never mind with other members of the population. If you take a more pragmatic view of the vote, which is simply to provide a means by which a group of people can exercise power within the term of a parliament, that can still be achieved with a market for votes. With the idea that democracy is justified because of the good of political participation, as well, it remains true that a lot of people do not vote. Even in polities such as Australia and Austria, where there is compulsory voting, there is a facility for people to register a 'no' vote

Equality and Corruption

or abstention, so there are limits on how far voting can be made intrinsically participative, even where it is made compulsory.

Then one might say that the marketisation of voting will somehow frustrate the will of the people. That would be a worry that some democratic theorists might voice. Obviously, I am going to skate over a lot of argument which has been set out in much more detail by my colleagues in political theory. However, the trouble with that argument is 'the people' looks like a chimera until it is effectuated by means of democratic procedures themselves. It seems like a remnant of magical thinking to invest the people, the demos, as the democratic sovereign, with personality, at least as divorced from the particular procedures which exist to give that will, hitherto inchoate, effect. So again, there is a certain disconcerting plasticity about the nature of the thing that is allegedly being denatured by the introduction of the vote.

Then there is the argument that is probably closest to what Sandel has in mind and also some of the positions that Debra Satz adopts in her book, which is that there is an intrinsic loss of value in introducing a market for votes. There is a depreciation, a corruption in that sense, in the very thought that you could trade votes for money among citizens. What libertarians may well want to say in response to that is, 'Yes, but somebody has to take a position about value.' Value again is not something that just drops out of the sky. It is always easy to understate the shallowness of deeply held convictions. Evaluative convictions can change dramatically in quite a short space of time, as we have seen with the gay marriage example that was discussed earlier. One reason for that is simply that people die with their deeply held evaluations and are replaced with people who do not have such deeply held evaluations. Beyond that, though, there is also the fact that in a pluralistic society people have different views about what is valuable. The libertarian response to that is: why do we not just cut to the chase and see what people will value through their market behaviour and, if they want to sell their vote to others, whether they are able to? If they do not want to sell it, they do not have to. They can still turn out and put the cross on the piece of paper when it comes to election time.

That, it seems to me, very quickly, is why the argument for corruption does not really do the job of refuting the proposal, or encounters certain problems. I am sure people will want to come back on some of the claims that have already been made.

I am now going to discuss the argument of fairness and see how well that does against the proposal. First of all, you can draw a distinction between vendors and buyers. Buyers may have a market standing of a certain kind, which differs from one agency to another. We are all familiar with that sort of possibility. Monopsony is one extreme version of that, where people's market domination can be used to extract lower prices on the market than in competitive markets, for example with large supermarket chains buying farmers' produce. That is true as far as it goes, but again who is going to decide whose market position is such as to give them undue influence over the ultimate price, in this case the price of the vote? There have to be questions answered then about what limits on market power there are; and, in principle, it is not clear whether these questions about market power are more intractable with regard to this example than with regard to some others, let us say.

The people who are selling votes, the electors, are they in an unfair position? You might say not, in the sense that everybody starts off equal. We all have one vote. I am assuming that the market would operate in a system in which there is a democratic franchise of one person, one vote. I was going to say more about this and then I decided that this would get us into technicalities. However, in a way this is close to the fantasy of Ronald Dworkin in his articles on equality, where he imagines people on a desert island.[8] They are given 100 clam-shells each and then they have to bid for goods in a market which includes insurance against certain, at that point unknown, liabilities. Dworkin's reason for this set-up is that it starts off from a baseline of equality. In other words, everyone has 100 clam-shells to start with and then there is a market between people who are endowed with equal resources to start with in terms of bidding for what bundles of goods they want at the end of the process. The reason why he wants to do this is because he thinks it is an undue imposition on people just to give them a one-size-fits-all bundle of indexed goods as, for example, Rawls did in *A Theory of Justice*. By contrast, for Dworkin, people ought to be able to decide rankings of goods for themselves. It ought to be ambition-sensitive, in the jargon, to how people tailor their particular favoured set of goods to their preference schedules.

Sometimes it is said that Dworkin is basing his argument there on the market, and that it is objectionable for that reason, but I do not think that is quite right. There is a market in there, but it is a market that is operated within a context of equality; one where each person is thought of as having equal resources to start with. It would be an entirely different situation if there were vast disparities in resource holdings to start with in terms of what came out.

It seems quite compelling from that point of view in the sense that we each have one vote to start with and we can then sell it. There will be differences in circumstances, because some constituencies are marginal, others are not. Therefore, the traded value of a particular vote would differ presumably from constituency to constituency depending on what the situation was, at least in any circumstances recognisably like those we have in the UK.

By reference to the values of equality, fairness and corruption in the abstract I have tried to suggest that the proposal to marketise voting, although seemingly outrageous, stands up, to a certain extent, against the criticisms one could extrapolate from what people like Sandel and Satz say. There is then the question, if that is right, what one might conclude from that. One conclusion, and this is a possible position, characteristic of some Oakeshottian conservatives, for example, could be simply that our political engagements go beyond our capacity to justify them rationally. If those are the best arguments, then perhaps that is the best we can do. That is what Russell says in the online interview with Debra Satz I mentioned earlier: his students, when this is put to them, react with outrage, but soon run out of arguments in trying to justify again some of their most fundamental democratic commitments as citizens.

I have tried to sketch the intuitive attractiveness, which also applies in other settings where market arguments are used, of an appeal to equality. The one point that I think does gain a lot of leverage is the fact that in practice this proposal would supervene on a set of circumstances where there are huge extant inequalities of market power. What tends to make libertarian positions less rebarbative than they might otherwise be is a tacit imagining away of these vast contours in, as it were, the landscape within which real markets tend to operate and would operate in a very foreseeable way if the system was introduced. The system starts in practice from a point markedly less egalitarian than the justifications I've looked at assume, and even from such a starting point its tendency is always (as Nozick argues) to disrupt that equality.

The final polemical point picks up on Steven's final remark too: the marketisation of voting does not look that much different from the way in which the electoral system in polities like the US and, increasingly, the UK operate, although in a formal sense we do not have a basis on which people can legally sell votes. It seems to me here, but also in areas that are further away from what is imaginable in current public policy terms than this one is, that advocacy of more marketising forms of argument rests on a form of utopianism.

Discussion

Richard Bronk
I really enjoyed both those presentations. One point I wanted to pick up is that it seems to me that the key aspect of commodification is rendering things commensurable. It seems to me that this offends us in two respects. One is the Isaiah Berlin point that key values are incommensurable and the deliberations and choices we make about how to weight those incommensurable choices define our identity and are the stuff of politics, not the markets. What the market therefore shares is the folly of utilitarianism, of believing that you can reduce values to a single scale of value or even commensurable values, in this case money, not utility. That seems to be the first point, that it offends our sense that there is incommensurability there, that there is no single scale of value and that it is a really deep identity-defining choice as to how we trade them off.

The second point though – and this is where I think the market is potentially much worse than utilitarianism – is the different weights given to different people in making that choice within a market. This picks up your final point, Glen. The point is that, in a market, rich people have the most money and so the weighting that is made by market-expressed preferences in terms of these choices is that the rich get the biggest say on what the value choice is. That is the other thing that offends us about the marketisation of certain aspects of the economy: we do not want the rich to have a bigger say about voting than the poor. That offends the basic notion of democracy.

Steven Lukes
I would like to say one thing about Isaiah Berlin. Of course, you are right that he is on to the issue of incommensurability and what he says can be very powerful. However, as I said, I think we are all hypocrites about this, and rightly so. We believe in Kant: pricelessness. We do not want things to be compared that should not be compared. We have strong feelings about this and yet, at the level of public policy, do you not agree we do want it to be done but we do not want to know about it? I think it is Schelling who says we should 'cut the Kant' (or is it 'cut the cant'?). We make these decisions all the time, for example when we make life insurance decisions.

Richard Bronk
Just because they are incommensurable does not mean you cannot have good reasons for the choices you make. It is just that there is not one right answer. That is his point.

Steven Lukes
Yes, but even Isaiah Berlin himself, later in his thinking about this, was prepared to talk about trade-offs. Perry noticed this, even in Kant himself. We talk as though there are sacred things that you cannot compare with one another and yet we do. I just think this is a case of hypocrisy.

Glen Newey
I think that what Steven has just said is right. Berlin's case for pluralism has received more attention than it probably deserved, at least as applied to policy decisions, because we do have to make these decisions all the time. The further question is if you emphasise the metaphysical plurality of value you still have to have a justification of value, including the justification of the metaphysical thesis, which is a philosophical question. However, when you come to public policy decisions you are going to have to couch the justification in some terms or other and the metaphysical thesis does not really give you the basis for doing that. You could still think, well, Berlin might be right about the incommensurability and hence plurality of value, but still think the common coin of political justification requires us to make decisions of the kind you mentioned with the *routes nationales* in terms of the foreseeable mortality from continuing to have scenic country roads in rural France.

Felix Martin
This reminds me very much of the debate about surely one of the most quantifiable areas of public policy. In the last 30 or 40 years monetary policy has had to be supported by an enormous range of very complicated models, which was not the case, say, before the Second World War. No one had any models at all to do monetary policy; it was all a question of judgement. I had an interesting discussion last summer with one of our leading monetary policy-makers here and I said, 'Has our monetary policy really got any better as a result of this? Why do you do it?' He said, 'No, no, no, of course not. The reason why we do this is not because we believe in any of these models. We know they are very deficient and we have just discovered, as a result of the last crisis,

they are even more deficient than we thought. However, in the current political environment, we have to be held accountable and therefore we need an apparatus of cost–benefit analysis, even though the decisions we make are matters of judgment as before.'

Robert H. Frank
I have a question for Glen Newey. Does not the most important objection to the buying and selling of votes arise from the free-rider problem? If you imagine a polluter who saves $1 million by being able to run a dirty process, and the process damages each of a million voters by $100, it sounds like a no-brainer that he should not run that process. However, if he offers them $5 each for their vote, each one knows that whether he accepts the $5 or not the outcome is going to be the same. There are so many voters, so why not accept the $5 and hope the others vote against it? However, if they accept it too, then I had better accept it just to hold my place in the purchasing power queue. I think that is a compelling reason not to allow people to sell their votes.

Glen Newey
I think that is a strong point about the free-rider problem, if you simply regard it as a bipartite transaction between two people. As with other cases where this form of argument is used, it just ignores externalities. It seems to me that at this level, which is the super-macro-level, what the externalities are going to be is itself one of the points that are up for debate. If you are buying a government, essentially, as a vote brokerage firm, one of the points that goes into the mix with politics is how far the conflict between incommensurable values can be resolved in a particular way in the public political sphere. Any system in which you are trying to put a cash value on trading, including allowance for externalities, is going

to prejudge that question. That is part of the problem. At the same time, part of the peculiar polemical forces of libertarian argument in this area, it seems to me, is that precisely because of the incommensurabilities there are different judgement calls that can be made, and then the reductive move – which says, well, okay, let us just ask people what the hell they want rather than trying to crunch the numbers for 60 million people – can come to look more compelling.

Robert H. Frank
The free-rider case has nothing whatsoever to do with incommensurability. In the example I was thinking of, it is 100 times more costly to dump the pollution than not and they can easily buy the votes necessary to enact that policy to everyone's detriment except the guy who buys the votes.

Glen Newey
Yes, sure. All I am saying is at the level of public policy formation you are going to get into questions of incommensurability, because if there is a clear pollutant, you might be able to put a cash value on that, but how do you put a cash value on, say, the marketisation of education in terms of social outcomes?

Showkat Ali
I have a request for clarification from Steven about your distinction between intrinsic and aggravating harm. The distinction itself is a bit ambiguous, because the concept of an intrinsic harm is ambiguous. So what work is the distinction doing?

Steven Lukes
This is a probing question and I have to say, as a defence, that it is a working distinction. It just seems to me to be the case that when we make claims about corruption

or commodification, we are appealing to some idea of the value, for example, of citizenship, which is not a value about citizenship in this or that context. It is a kind of general claim. Whereas if we talk about the harm done by buying and selling sexual services, we are asking: 'What harm does it do in a given context?' I do not claim any deep foundation for this distinction. It just seemed to me that it works differently in those two kinds of argument.

Jonathan Derbyshire
You Steven made two criticisms of Sandel. One is that he does not choose his examples of corruption carefully enough and, two, that for some of them you would feel much less badly than others.

Steven Lukes
Yes.

Jonathan Derbyshire
I do not feel particularly badly about Skyboxes at baseball stadia.

Steven Lukes
Or paying children to read, which seems to me to be rather a good idea.

Jonathan Derbyshire
The more powerful objection is precisely connected to the idea of intrinsic harm, because I took you to be arguing the fact that the very notion of intrinsic harms is incoherent.

Steven Lukes
No, I do not think that. Well, it depends how much weight you want to put on 'intrinsic'. What I am saying is that it is really difficult to dispute some kinds of harm. For example, if friends start to decide how much each of them is paying for the next round of beer or something, that

makes you wonder whether they know what friendship is. That seems to me to be a compelling claim and I do not see how you can doubt that. Of course, you can always then say that the concept of friendship varies from one context to another.

Robert Skidelsky
Samuelson, in that best-selling textbook,[9] explains the process by which a group of friends sharing a flat should, logically, divide up their labour. A is better than B at both cleaning and washing up, but he is worse at washing up than cleaning, so he should concentrate on cleaning and leave washing up to B. This is the famous theory of comparative advantage. But perhaps he did not understand friendship.

Steven Lukes
I do think Zelizer's book is very interesting about this, because what she shows is that, in reality, money is intimately bound up in lots of intimate relationships and we do not recognise this.

Véronique Munoz-Dardé
I have a question for Steven. You said something about the areas in which you think that something negative happens when you introduce money. You just mentioned it in passing, and I was not quite sure what was happening, so I wanted to ask you. If I think of places where you pay for your education and places where you do not, it is not obvious to me that the introduction of money degrades education. It would only do so if it changed our students into consumers.

Steven Lukes
Then we have to go into some complex detail. Just paying is not the point. It is the question of marketing and I suppose then we have to talk about privatising, which

raises other kinds of questions, profit and so on, and I did not get into all of that. In the most advanced capitalist country, America, there is a complete commitment to public education. It is often not very good, but the idea that you could privatise it all is not on the cards. Why? It is because you need to have public instruction, civic values and so on. That is recognised there. In other words, it is not just about paying for education; it is the idea that provision of educational services could be left up to the market, which seems to me not compatible with citizenship.

Jonathan Derbyshire
The harm done would be an aggravated harm.

Steven Lukes
Yes. I have not worked this out, I have to tell you, but I think that citizenship is a point where the corruption and the inequality argument come together.

David Graeber
It strikes me that the question of incommensurable values is way overstated. It seems to me that most of our lives and most ordinary decisions are of making compromises between incommensurable values. Every time you decide what to make for dinner you are deciding between healthiness, ease of preparation, taste. These are formally incommensurable values and we do it all the time, so I do not think that is essentially a problem.

When we get into the larger picture, why is money different from other forms of value? I am going to make a semi-Marxist argument here that has to do with the commoditisation of labour. We work for money. Money is the form in which our action is returned to us as a value form. Every time you hear people talk about 'values', first of all, family values: what is the major form of uncommoditised labour? It is housework. Art, religion, wherever you have some zone of uncommoditised labour, that is where people talk about values, but those values are considered to be valuable because they are incommensurable. Therefore, in one case, the form of value of money is valuable because it has fungibility, because it is comparable. The other way, it is valuable because it is not. Obviously there is going to be a contradiction when you try to move between one and the other. Politics is the formal art of mediating publicly between incommensurable values at a social level. That is the reason, it strikes me, that marketising politics seems particularly obnoxious, because that is the alternative way to do it.

Steven Lukes
You remind me irresistibly of Max Weber's essay on politics as a vocation, where he says just this, but his view is probably more dramatic than yours. He thinks that politics is a standoff between people saying 'here is where I stand' and there is no way of bridging the gap. I do not think it is really like that. We usually trade off for a reason and a metric is useful, especially if we are talking about administration.

Richard Seaford
I thought the key issue was the brief moment when Glen Newey gave us the schmoctoring argument, which you glossed over very quickly as if you thought Nozick had a point. It seems as if the schmoctoring argument is at the heart of the whole issue, and it certainly relates to the power of money. Incidentally, it seems to be the worst kind of professorial hypothesising, a kind of sophistry, which is going to impress almost nobody, I would have thought. Well, perhaps it does impress academics. What really is at stake in the schmoctoring argument is the idea that there is a kind of activity called money-making,

which is in parallel to all other kinds of activity. However, most people would say that the goal of doctoring is health and if it is diminished by money-making then so much the worse for money-making. That would be a perfectly normal position. Aristotle deals with precisely this issue. He even mentions doctoring and says that if you are a doctor, you can do it for a human good or you can do it to make money. Aristotle says that money-making is unnatural because the final cause of human activity is a human good. Money, because it is unlimited, falls outside nature; it is not a human good. Therefore, it is quite different from everything else. Money can be a means to a human good, but it is not a human good and money-making is unnatural because it does not have a final cause.

You may think using metaphysics is a bit abstruse when we are dealing with these issues of the current economy, but Aristotelian ethics has made an enormous comeback in the last ten or fifteen years, partly for reasons of this kind. I would also say that the influence of Aristotle on Marx is enormous. There is a book by Scott Meikle,[10] which I do not think has been mentioned yet, which explains how Marx's Aristotelian education on these issues, the issue of the metaphysics of money, is absolutely central to Marxism. We cannot avoid Aristotle and I certainly would rate Aristotle over Nozick on this particular point.

Glen Newey
I am sure we all prefer Aristotle to Nozick if you have to plump for one or the other. It seems to me that the polemical force of Nozick is simply to debunk an internal goal argument, which is not necessarily the same as the basic human goods argument. You can find both of those kinds of metaphysics in Aristotle. However, it is going to be quite hard to justify public policy outcomes

by reference to the fourfold typology of *teloi* in Aristotle. There is then a debate to be had, for example about what the good of medicine consists in and what curative goals consist in. That is going to have quite strong implications for what resources are allocated to what kinds of activity.

John Milbank
I am slightly worried that everything being said about money is correct, but we are losing sight of the fact that similar things can be said about technology, bureaucratisation and rationalisation. This was brought home to me in Steven Lukes's paper, where at one point he said 'depersonalisation of medicine is good' and then he said 'but in America it is getting too depersonalised because of money'. I am totally with you on what is happening in America, but we also need to criticise the extent to which all medicine nowadays is no longer about the human good and is subject to exponential increases of demand to delay death, get rid of pain, with the endless invention of new diseases and so on. We really need to move back to a much more interpersonal mode of medicine. We need to know about your whole life, your whole story, not just what is happening inside your body. It is very significant that the British Association of Psychologists has just said that it is sceptical about so-called psychological diseases and their classification and it would be much better if doctors dealing with mental health dealt with people's social relationships, their existential conditions and so on.

My challenge to you, then, is if you are going to criticise depersonalisation of medicine in America, should you not be rather more critical about the whole process of modern medicine, the whole depersonalisation and rationalisation of modern medicine, because the same problems with money are also problems with technology and bureaucracy?

Steven Lukes
That is a whole bundle of questions. I was making a somewhat narrower point about medicine. Some aspects of marketisation have to be good. The extent to which it is encouraging patients to attend to their own health and put fewer burdens on the doctors has good consequences to some extent. It is a very mixed story, but essentially you are right: this is a perfect Baumol good. The best medical practice involves time, attention and specific attention to the individual and that is a human good, unquestionably.

Notes

1. Michael Sandel, *What Money Can't Buy: The Moral Limits of Markets* (London: Penguin, 2013); Debra Satz, *Why Some Things Shouldn't Be For Sale: The Moral Limits of Markets* (Oxford: OUP, 2012).
2. Margaret Radin, *Contested Commodities* (Cambridge, MA: Harvard University Press, 1996).
3. Viviana Zelizer, *Pricing the Priceless Child: The Changing Social Value of Children* (Princeton: Princeton University Press, 1994); *The Purchase of Intimacy* (Princeton: Princeton University Press, 2007).
4. K. Polanyi, *The Great Transformation: The Political and Economic Origins of Our Time*, 2nd edn (Boston: Beacon Press, 2001).
5. T H Marshall, *Citizenship and Social Class, and Other Essays* (Cambridge: Cambridge University Press, 1950)
6. See www.econtalk.org/archives/2011/08/satz_on_markets.html.
7. Robert Nozick, *Anarchy, State and Utopia* (New York: Basic Books, 1974).
8. Ronald Dworkin, *Sovereign Virtue: The Theory and Practice of Equality* (Cambridge, MA: Harvard University Press, 2002).
9. Paul Samuelson, *Economics: An Introductory Analysis* (New York: McGraw-Hill, 1948).
10. Scott Meikle, *Aristotle's Economic Thought* (Oxford: Clarendon Press, 1997).

Session 3

The Moral Limits of Markets

Edward Skidelsky

This is going to be a continuation of the discussion before lunch. In that discussion we heard about two different arguments, or kinds of argument, for calling a market 'noxious': an argument from equality and an argument from corruption. A market can be called noxious because it undermines human equality, either because some of its participants are vulnerable to exploitation or because it inflicts serious harms on some section of the population. Alternatively, a market can be called noxious because it *corrupts* the good it traffics in, by imposing on it a meaning that is not properly its own. Modern liberals are generally uncomfortable with this latter argument, because it implies, unpalatably from their point of view, that a voluntary, victim-free transaction can nonetheless be vicious. I want to defend the corruption argument, both because I think it is a valid argument and also because I think it is primarily a worry about corruption, and not equality, that underlies our fear of creeping marketisation. Here, as elsewhere, modern liberalism imposes a kind of hypocrisy on us. It forces us to voice our moral intuitions in a language alien to them.

I want to focus on the example of prostitution, which Steven Lukes has already touched on. Prostitution is not just a noxious market; it is the very prototype of a noxious market. We talk of scientists and writers 'prostituting' themselves for money. We describe actions and arguments as 'meretricious', from the Latin *meretricius*, 'of or pertaining to prostitutes'. Prostitution can therefore serve as a specimen case. If our objection to it is based on concerns about corruption, not inequality, the same may be equally true of other noxious markets.

As we heard earlier, Debra Satz has tried to explain the badness of prostitution using an equality-style argument. According to her, prostitution is not bad in itself but because it helps to sustain, as a matter of contingent fact, 'a social world in which women form a subordinated social group'. Perhaps it does. However, this does not get to the root of our objection to prostitution for two reasons. First, as Satz herself admits, her argument applies only to the sale of sex by women. It does not apply to the sale of sex by *men*, either to women or to other men. This looks arbitrary. It also poses a tricky legislative problem. Either we restrict prostitution in general – male and female – which seems hard on male prostitutes and their clients, who do not contribute in any way to the subordination of women; or we restrict only female prostitution, which flies in the face of many UN and EU anti-discrimination conventions.

However, the more fundamental objection to Satz's argument is that it doesn't cut deep enough. Satz thinks that the reason prostitution contributes to the negative stereotyping of women is that a large number of people think that it is 'especially objectionable'. She treats this belief as a bare sociological fact. She does not question whether it is true or not. But clearly, the fact that many people regard prostitution as objectionable only carries moral force if prostitution is indeed objectionable: otherwise, the correct response is 'get over it'. Consider a structurally similar argument about miniskirts. Many conservative-minded people regard miniskirts as objectionable. The wearing of miniskirts therefore contributes to the negative stereotyping of women. But we do not think that miniskirts should therefore be banned or regulated, because we (the right-thinking liberals to whom this kind of argument is addressed) do not think there is anything particularly wrong with them, and we regard the objection to them as a prejudice to be overcome. It is because we *don't* think this way about prostitution – don't really think this way, whatever we say on the subject – that Satz's argument seems to us plausible. It trades on moral intuitions that it cannot acknowledge.

This drives us back to the corruption argument. What does it mean in general, leaving aside prostitution for the moment, to say that marketising a practice corrupts it? As Steven said, it can mean a number of things. I want to focus on one particular meaning of corruption. I want to say that marketising a practice corrupts it by altering the practice's internal goal, transforming it into another inferior kind of practice. Michael Sandel, in his book *What Money Can't Buy*,[1] gives the example of 'Shakespeare in the Park'. This free theatrical project in New York Central Park is increasingly monopolised by the rich, who secure tickets by paying others to stand in line for them. As Sandel points out, it is not clear from an economic point of view what is wrong with this. If a rich person wants to pay a poor person to take his place in a queue, then both people presumably benefit and no one else suffers. It is Pareto efficient, in the jargon. Nevertheless, the effect of this has been to transform 'Shakespeare in the Park' from a civic celebration, an affirmation of shared citizenship, into an ordinary consumption item. The performances remain the same, but their social meaning has been corrupted. Sandel extends a similar kind of argument to many other practices.

But why talk about corruption here, as opposed simply to change? The implication of the term 'corruption' is that human practices and institutions have a meaning built into them, alteration of which constitutes a falling-off or degradation. This archaic-sounding notion is rejected by most modern liberals. They say, 'surely our practices and institutions will bear whatever meaning we choose to give them? They have no essential or built-in meaning, deviation from which could count as corruption'. To revert to Nozick's example, which Glen Newey referred to: a doctor accused of prostituting his talents for pay might simply retort that he is in the business not of 'doctoring' but of 'schmoctoring' – which is just like doctoring, except that its internal goal is to earn money for the 'schmoctor'. I think this is a bit of a cheap shot. A doctor who strives to maximise his income by giving patients whatever drugs they ask for, or by performing useless operations on the sick and desperate, is not engaged in some alternative practice of 'schmoctoring'; he is simply a bad doctor. The internal goal of medicine is health, not profit: no individual or society is free to stipulate otherwise. In this I agree with Bernard Williams against Nozick. This is what is meant by calling medicine a profession as opposed to a trade.

This point can be generalised. Many, not all, human practices have an inherent, as opposed to a merely stipulated, goal, meaning that we can sensibly talk about them being corrupted. I want to demonstrate this using the particular example of prostitution. Sex, like doctoring, has an inherent purpose or telos that is corrupted when it is put up for sale. We do not have to conceive of this purpose very ambitiously. We do not have to make out that the inherent function of sex is procreation – the traditional Catholic natural law view – or the affirmation of long-term loving relationships – the romantic view. In fact what I have to say about the normal sexual act applies just as much to casual, loveless encounters as it does to procreative or passionate couplings. But it is enough to reveal prostitution as a corruption.

I want to say three things about the normal sexual act, and I stress that by 'normal' I mean not just 'usual' but 'in accordance with the norm'; this is not a purely statistical notion. First, the normal sexual act is an expression of sexual desire. By this, I do not just mean that it aims to satisfy sexual desire, in the way that eating typically aims to satisfy hunger. The relationship is more intimate than that. I mean that sex *expresses* sexual desire, in the same sort of way as a smile expresses happiness or weeping expresses grief. The relationship is an expressive one; it is not just a means to an end. This is why having sex without desire seems to us fake or phoney, in a way that eating without hunger (to please your host, say) does not. It is fake or phoney in the same way that laughing without mirth is fake, or weeping without grief.

Second, sexual desire – the desire that the sexual act normally expresses – is not just a desire for another person's body, but a desire for his or her desiring body. Montaigne put it very nicely. He said, 'what must be courted and ensnared is the will. I am horrified by the thought of a body given to me but lacking love'. The whole psychological interest of sexual desire – as opposed to, say, a desire for food or drink – lies in this reflexive structure. It is a desire for a desiring subject, not simply a desire for an object. Hence the intimate entanglement of sex and power, a theme explored by Sartre, and many others.

Indeed, the reciprocity involved in sexual desire – and this is my third point – is even more complex than Montaigne's remarks suggest, for what is desired is not just another person's desire but another person's desire as responsive to one's own desire. Now this is a bit hard to get one's head around, but a device proposed by

Thomas Nagel helps. Imagine, he wrote, a man gazing with desire through a mirror at a woman who is gazing with desire at him. He is aware of her gaze, which further inflames his desire, but she is not aware of his gaze. Were she to notice his gaze, and he to notice its effect on her, this would add a further dimension to his desire. After this, Nagel adds, 'it becomes difficult to imagine further iterations, though they may be logically distinct'.

These three features describe the normal sexual act. How does sex for money differ? We can approach the matter from the point of view either of the prostitute or her client. (For convenience, I will say 'she' when referring to the prostitute and 'he' when referring to the client, but what I say is equally applicable to all possible combinations.) A woman who has sex for money is not usually, I take it, expressing sexual desire. She is, of course, trying to satisfy another kind of desire, a desire for money, but she is not directly expressing this desire in the sexual act. The sexual act is, as we say, a mere means to an end. Could she achieve this end in some other, more agreeable way, she would. This instrumental use of a normally expressive act involves a kind of self-objectification, a self-objectification akin to, though much deeper than, that of the airline hostess, with her perpetually fixed smile. It is meretricious, in both the original and the extended sense of the word. There are of course some prostitutes – not many I suspect, but some – who enjoy their jobs, and I will come back to them in a moment.

What about the client? For him, intercourse is of course an expression of sexual desire. Only his desire is not desire for another's desire, because he knows full well – unless he is very deluded – that the prostitute does not desire him. It is a desire for a mere body, a piece of flesh. The feelings of the prostitute are a matter of indifference to him. Montaigne thought there was something disgusting, something almost necrophiliac, about such a desire; he actually compares it to necrophilia. However, there is another logical possibility, which is that the client is not merely indifferent to the feelings of the prostitute, but positively aroused by the thought that she is yielding to him unwillingly, under the pressure of economic need. In this case, his motive is a sadistic one. He derives sexual pleasure from his power to inflict pain or discomfort. So the relationship between female prostitution and misogyny is not merely accidental, as Satz claims, but essential. It is hard to imagine a society in which prostitutes were simply treated as providers of a service – sex workers, sex therapists – on a par with hairdressers. A form of indifference or contempt is actually built into the relationship.

What about the willing prostitute, the prostitute who enjoys her job? Here there is both sexual desire and reciprocity, but this reciprocity is importantly incomplete. The willing prostitute is aroused by her client's arousal, but she is not aroused – how could she be, for there is no such thing – by her client's arousal at her arousal. Indeed, the opposite is more likely. She is aroused by the thought of his indifference or contempt. What we have here, in other words, is masochism, a sexual pleasure derived from humiliation. I am speculating. This is unfamiliar territory for me. But something of this sort must be the case, because where the reciprocal structure of desire is complete, the money just drops out as irrelevant – in fact, it becomes an impediment. At this point it would be natural for her to say to him, 'You don't need to bother with that.' As long as the money is there, then it stands in the way of the completion of this reciprocal structure of desire.

In short, paying for sex changes the essential nature of the act. It either transforms what is normally an expression of desire into a mere means to an end, or else it changes the character of the desire itself, rending it animalistic or perverted, or it does both things at once, depending on which of the two parties you look at. Prostitution is the corruption of sex by money and it is this, not any inequalities that it sustains, that constitutes its particular badness. Note that this account I have given you does not presuppose anything about the essential nature of men or women; it is equally applicable to gay prostitution or the prostitution of men for female clients. It is gender-indifferent. Satz claims in her book that essentialist accounts of the badness of prostitution presuppose certain theories of male and female nature. I am not doing anything like that.

It is doubtless because sex is so basic to human life, and so universal, that prostitution has become a symbol of monetary corruption in general. This is why, as well as its intrinsic interest, I have chosen it as an example. But I could have chosen other examples. Teaching, doctoring, science, the administration of justice: all of these activities have, like sex, an inherent goal or telos, which can be corrupted by being subordinated to the money motive. Of course, the precise form of corruption will vary from activity to activity. My remarks on corruption are not intended to be applicable across the board; they merely aim to suggest a general form of argument. It would be interesting to see how you might develop a similar argument for some of these other human practices.

Let me return to medicine, which we discussed briefly earlier. What the good doctor is aiming at is not simply the satisfaction of his or her client's wants, because those wants may be based on misinformation, irrational phobias and so forth, but the *health* of his or her client. He wants to do what he judges is in the best interest of his client, regardless of his client's wants. That is why the want-satisfaction model, the economic model, is not applicable to medicine. I would say something similar about education. The good teacher is not simply aiming to satisfy his or her students' wants, because those wants may be vague, distorted or open-ended. No, the teacher tries to teach what he or she judges is in the best interest of the student to learn. Here again, the introduction of a consumer model – the notion of education as an 'enhancement of the student experience', etc. – is corrupting of the practice, and has been very destructive in British universities.

There are some interesting problem cases that I will just touch on in conclusion. Land, I think, was mentioned earlier. This was one of Polanyi's 'fictitious commodities'. The idea goes back to Coleridge: land is not properly a commodity; that is the wrong way to value land. What about manufacture? Does manufacture have a telos that can be corrupted by money? Ruskin famously thought it did. He argued, rather heroically, that the true craftsman would rather starve than produce a shoddy item. Most modern thinkers are quite happy to see the money motive prevail here. 'General Motors is not in the business of making cars,' remarked its CEO Thomas Murphy. 'It is in the business of making money.' Underlying this remark is the optimistic assumption that, in aiming to make money, General Motors will also necessarily aim to make good cars. I see no reason to believe this. On the contrary, it seems to me likely that an overriding interest in profit will induce manufacturers to take shortcuts wherever possible, reckoning the loss of a few discerning customers well worth the gain of many more undiscerning ones. If this is so, then there is a real tension between the craft ethos on the one hand and the profit motive on the other. In that case, we can talk of the corruption of manufacturing by money, very much in the spirit of Ruskin and William Morris and so forth.

I would be interested to know what economics has to say about this. I assume not much, because orthodox economics does not recognise the money motive as a distinct kind of motive – it is just subsumed under the general notion of utility maximisation. But that is an indictment of economics, because clearly there *is* a distinction, sociological and psychological, between one manufacturer whose aim is to make things and to make them well and another manufacturer for whom making things is merely auxiliary to the goal of making money. That is a distinction we all recognise. It is a problem with modern economics if it cannot articulate that distinction.

John Milbank

Robert and Edward's book, *How Much Is Enough?*, focused on the question of moral limits to the market. I think one needs to have that focus. There is something inherently dangerous about money, inherently dangerous about the market, as we keep saying today. To some degree, the economy is a kind of feral monster that you need to keep at bay.

Nonetheless, I do think there is another question to be asked: How far is this a monster that can be tamed? In other words, the question is: Can you have moral markets? I want to approach this question, first of all, genealogically, by asking it the other way around. Why have we got the idea that somehow the economy and the market and morality are naturally averse to each other? Some of the things that people have already said today about other economies have suggested that this is an extremely peculiar view. I think it is useful to start by distinguishing between the marketplace on the one hand and the market on the other. By marketplace I mean any kind of process of exchange, which may be in terms of very fixed moral values and very fixed understandings of people's place in the social hierarchy and what they can expect. We should distinguish marketplace exchanges on the one hand – which often are linked to a specific physical site – from market exchanges on the other hand, in the modern capitalist sense, where what we mean by a market is that they undergo clearance in terms of the matching of supply with demand.

That second sense of market is unusual. It has characterised the West increasingly since the 18th century. We cannot, I think, see it as something natural. There would be no reason to think that. We have to see it as, in Polanyi's terms, being both embedded and instituted. Polanyi says that we think that the society is embedded in the economy but he also carries on thinking that even a capitalist economy is in fact embedded in a certain anthropology, a certain notion of the human being, a certain sense of society and a certain sense of what the business of legislation is. I think our economy has also been instituted. Just because somehow the supply and demand mechanism seems to work automatically we have the delusion that this is natural and not actually embedded in a set of social and political practices.

What then are the big differences between this and the pre-modern marketplace? First of all, as Steven Lukes, following Polanyi, has mentioned, some things were sacred; some things were not exchanged; some things could not even enter into gift exchange. We can think of people, land and money itself as things which should not be exchanged or speculated upon. We can usefully ask ourselves how far we still obey the sacralities in a completely secularised world. We certainly do not see land as sacred any more, and I would suggest that, despite the abolition of slavery, we really do in all kinds of ways, and appallingly, exchange people.

But beyond this point that in a traditional economy certain things just could not be exchanged – so in Polanyi's sense, were not economies – we can also say that, even where things were exchanged, they were mainly exchanged in terms of reciprocity and respect for preceding social hierarchies. You can see this, for example, in Aristotle's account, and so things that were exchanged were then not commodities in Marx's sense. They were not subordinating use value to exchange value. That, as has already been said, was profoundly linked to the business of mutual recognition that the economy did not break with; rather it went along with a process of recognising who people were, recognising their honour, their trade, what they needed to fulfil themselves and so on. I think it is correct that, in most societies, people have been hobbits. They want respectability in the Shire, but all societies have known that there are some maniacs; there are some incredibly dangerous people, who would like to go off and work for Saruman, for example. Most societies have thought that you have to ward off the danger of those people. Thus primitive societies have inbuilt safeguards to guard against risk, and what is strange about our world is that we have almost built it on the abolition of these safeguards. We have made a Faustian pact, as the Skidelskys have so very well said.

Here I think it is really important to cite the evidence of a lot of recent medieval and early modern historians who suggest that, in the initial phase of the development of Western technology, the growth of an urban and a monetary economy was not necessarily going in a capitalist direction; that right up to early modernity, in fact, processes of reciprocity, elements of gift exchange, were being reinforced through this urban economy. Liberals and Marxists are equally guilty of not historicising enough, in my view, and not seeing the sheer contingency of the

Western development. It is not that the West was the first to get to capitalism, as if everybody was bound to get there. It's much more a case of why. Why on earth did the West do something as peculiar as capitalism? In my view, that is the question. I think that increasingly the evidence suggests that this process has got to do with religion. It has got to do with Christianity and what happened to Christianity.

First of all, as Ivan Illich liked to point out, the story of the Good Samaritan is uniquely significant. In Jesus's parable, we have a case of somebody exercising friendship totally outside national and cultural boundaries. What that did was set up a dynamic of free association in the West. People stepped out of their communities quite quickly. They formed monasteries, they formed new organic communities, and yet this happened outside any given ethnic communities. This went way beyond what happened in the antique city.

The second thing that is specific to Christianity, as has recently been discussed by the Italian philosopher Giorgio Agamben[2] and by many other people as well, is the extraordinary way in which Christianity extended the cash group, the *oikos*, or household, to the political sphere. The Church itself thought of itself as an *oikos*; not only that, the divine providential government of the world was described as an *oikonomia*. Not really any longer as a *politeia*. An *oikonomia* means that you have the sort of very detailed concern for everybody's very specific wellbeing that a father would have for his family. Foucault's explanation of pastoral rule and the bio-political clearly occupies this space also. What is extraordinary about the Christian sense of *oikonomia* is that it begins with the sense that there is an abundance of divine grace that is adapting itself to our finite needs. This is exactly the opposite of what we have come to think of as the economic, where we have infinite needs but the resources are scarce. This is precisely an inversion of the original meaning, in theology, of *oikonomia*. I think that this is absolutely crucial to our self-understanding and what has happened in modernity.

Now, what I think has happened could be described as a kind of perversion of this Christian legacy. Ivan Illich talks about the institutionalisation of charity which has turned into bureaucracy, or, on the other hand, these relations at a distance, in which relations with a stranger become completely indifferent to charity altogether. On one hand, there is a very nannyish kind of bureaucracy; on the other hand, a totally indifferent, totally amoral market. But we really only arrive at the modern sense of the economic – and people like Jean-Claude Michéa and other researchers in Paris have shown this[3] – through Jansenism, because the Jansenists, like the Calvinists, thought that we are totally depraved, so it is impossible to produce a human society on the basis of morality. They have the idea that divine government works through our vices, it distils an order out of our vices. This is characteristic also of some French Huguenot thought; it is no accident that Bernard de Mandeville is a Huguenot in exile, so you get *Private Vices, Public Benefits*. Hence, the model that is transposed in more naturalistic terms by Adam Smith is theological: how divine government works.

What is really peculiar about our legacy is, on the one hand, it is a very hedonistic model – we just deal with people's material desires – but this model also belongs to a certain kind of gloomy piety or theology. The Conservative Party is still this alliance between those kind of Christians on the one hand and cynical City hedonists on the other hand. We are still living through this legacy. Despite that – and this will be far too complicated to go into now – it would not be true to say that political economy got totally amoralised until we get to the phenomenon of marginalism, which, as the Skidelskys and others have so well said, does not assume any objective teleology. It is a rational choice theory; you have all sorts of choices that you pursue according to a utilitarian instrumentality, which also assumes a scarcity, so it has finally lost any belief in God – economic belief in divine grace or the abundance of creation. It assumes, on the contrary, a rather mean, scarce nature. Essentially that is because there is no human *telos* any longer. Our desires are infinite and various and therefore, inevitably, there is not going to be enough to go around.

The opposite of this – and here I totally agree with everything Edward Skidelsky has said – has to be some kind of invocation of new dimensions of *eudaimonia* in the Aristotelian sense; some sense of objective human flourishing. In other words, if there is a scale of values, then there can be something more like sufficiency; the really worthwhile goods like marriage and children and a fulfilling task you have to perform, and enjoying where you live – these are not so subject to these marginalist criteria. Indeed, I think one of the problems with modern economics is that it misdescribes what is going on. In some ways, I think the political left needs to consider the idea that we have never been quite as capitalist as we think. Just as Bruno Latour says, 'we have never been modern'. We too easily imagine that everything does happen, even nowadays, according to capitalist norms, but to some degree it does not because people still have a kind of Orwellian common sense, I think. Jon Cruddas has recently said on the radio that he thinks that the choice for the British Labour Party will be whether it sticks with an economistic model or decides to put the issue of human flourishing centre stage.

As an appendage to that important remark by Jon Cruddas, I want to make some remarks to finish with about the history of socialism in relation to economics; I am not sure anybody has said quite what I am going to say here, before. I think socialism basically has gone in three stages. To begin with socialism was a profoundly anti-economic doctrine, precisely because it assumed that the economic was defined in the way that the political economists had defined it. The early socialists tended to see socialism and cooperation in production as alternatives to any kind of economic exchange because they assumed that that was an amoral sphere. Even Marx, in a sense, is imagining a future in which exchange will have gone – exchange with nature or exchange with other human beings – and there will be a pure utopia of productivity. After 1890, we have the birth of economistic socialism, in which overwhelmingly the Left – whether we are talking about Fabians in England, or eventually the people behind the Iron Curtain – accept marginalism, and accept the logic of rational calculation. This is the sense in which the Skidelskys' book is possibly creating a new line of division in politics – what wasn't there before. Many researchers have pointed out that the invisible hand of the market or the visible hand of the state can both operate in terms of rational utility. Indeed, sometimes when neoliberals were modelling the perfect market they used the socialist state as an example to think what it would be like, because in a sense the state is like God and it is God that stands behind the idea of the invisible hand. Therefore even when we have market socialism in Yugoslavia and the idea of common property, sometimes this was presented in terms of 'this will better realise a perfect Smithean free market in terms of goods other than labour if you leave labour as fixed'.

I think that there has been a dreadful failure on all sides of the political spectrum to challenge this idea, that the economy is necessarily immoral. There is a big contrast to this, as has been pointed out by Italian economists, particularly Bruni and Zamagni.[4] They have argued that the Italian tradition of civil economy never quite accepted this way of looking at things. The big thinker here is Smith's predecessor, Antonio Genovesi, pupil of Giambattista Vico in Naples. The point of contrast with Smith is that whereas Smith has sympathy in the social realm he does not quite get sympathy inside the economic contract itself. Very simply, and famously, you and your butcher do not care about each other's welfare when you are making a transaction. That is the point of difference with the Italian political economic tradition: they think that, because the butcher is also your neighbour, you care.

This relates to what Steven Lukes has written about how we are often not just making money. Familial, local and neighbourly transactions can involve an economic element, but they are interwoven with each other. This has been much truer of the Italian tradition, which has gone on in continuity with an Aristotelian and a Catholic legacy, thinking that the contract itself can be a site of social negotiation. In other words, you are not just going for what independently you want but you are also trying to work out what would be fair between you. This is a perfectly viable model. I would submit that the Anglo-Saxon world has less of that in practice than many parts of the Continent, which still continue to have that as a tacit assumption behind the ways they do things.

What I want to recommend is a third socialism, which would be an economy society socialism. That would be a socialism that would see the economy as fully part of civil society and would try to redesign the economic contract itself. It would be a socialism less inimical to exchange, if you like. It would be bringing a kind of Maussian perspective into dialogue with Marx and other socialist figures.

Of course, Karl Polanyi is precisely the person who began to do this. His relationship to Mauss is very strong.

This runs into the entire question of agency. I do not know the answer here, but I think that what these labels like 'Red Tory', 'Blue Labour' and 'One Nation Labour' are all groping towards is a new paradoxical fusion of a greater participatory democracy on the one hand with some elements of high Tory paternalism on the other hand. In other words, we break with the paradigms of the past by saying that we need real moral repentance by our leaders and we need to restore a sense of honour. At the same time, we need to embed that at a popular level, with ordinary people getting much more involved in their lives. How can this happen? It can only happen when people start to pursue different practices; when they start, as Phillip Blond has argued, to pursue recognition in terms of honour, and then gradually this becomes more attractive.

The re-embedding of the economic has to happen both at the level of ethos and simultaneously at the level of legislation – from above and below at the same time. We need a change in company law that would insist that every company pursues a social purpose. If you are making cars you are making cars and not just making money; you are making money but you are also making cars. We need vocational entry requirements for almost every profession and trade and some kind of restoration of a guild process, which the Labour Party recently seemed to be thinking about. We need a sharing of risk between investors and owners, shareholders and managers, lenders and borrowers, and employers and employees. If we are going to have a market exchange, let us have genuinely fair market exchange and competition. We also need, besides the participation of workers in businesses, a certain backing-up by courts of the questions of prices, wages and interest on loans. That has to come within the jurisdiction of courts to some degree. They have to be able to lay down certain boundaries.

Now, all this seems well-nigh impossible. I am not saying it is possible. Nonetheless, I do think that one can plausibly argue that an ethical economy will be a more stable and more viable economy. A lot of firms – even places like Walmart – are discovering that if you are too uprooted and do not care about your communities at all, in the long term that has a negative consequence.

The paradox of social benefit thinking is that you have to pursue it sincerely. If people do not really want to pursue social benefit they will cut corners. Nonetheless, if you sincerely pursue social benefit as well as economic benefit it will have more stable, longterm economic benefits. The big question then is: How can good practice drive out bad practice? Sometimes bad practice is advantageous; other times good practice is. In the long term, good practice is more stable in market terms. How can we demonstrate that and make this more attractive?

The other reason why I think an ethical economy is more stable and beneficial is that it does stop the conflict identified by Marx between labour and capital, between supply and demand, between a situation where people will endlessly demand more wages on one side and on the other side people are endlessly pursuing as much profit as they can extract. Of course, it is from the conflict between those things – and this is the straight Marxist element in what I am saying – that we still have endemic crises and cycles. You can only stop those at the point where people accept that the transactions they are involved in are in fact fair and just.

Discussion

Geoffrey Hosking

Thank you very much for a fascinating speech John, and it is good to have some history brought in to this discussion; it has been rather absent so far. Thank you also for reminding us that markets have moral elements in them. They are not necessarily immoral; not all markets anyway. I want to suggest that there is an essentially moral feature about markets, which can perhaps be mobilised to reduce the immorality of them. The modern capitalist market depends, to a much greater extent than in previous society, on investment. If you are investing money in a company or a firm it is because you think it is going to be stable and it is going to make you some money. You are giving the firm credit and credit is the financial term for trust. One of the essential elements of a market economy is trust. It is actually not just trust, but trust in the trustworthy. It is absolutely crucial that you have both terms, because a lot of trust is misplaced. That element of the market needs to be strengthened and revived against other elements of the market, which I am going to talk about in an hour or so – the dangers of money within the market.

Richard Bronk

I just wanted to make two points in this fascinating discussion. One, since this is a Skidelsky occasion, is a Keynes point, but Schumpeter said something similar. That is that maybe we have been living in a long-phase transition between the religious era and the very non-religious era, and capitalism worked best when we were in that phase transition. Virginia Woolf has an entry in her diary where Keynes expresses this: 'We had the best of both worlds. We destroyed Christianity and yet had its benefits.'[5] That was a very neat way of putting it. There was a point when we had the legacy of Christianity and the dynamism of markets at the same time. Is part of what is happening that this balance has disappeared?

I also wanted to pick up on something that Edward said, which is about companies defining their goals entirely in terms of money or profit. This comes back to the commensurability argument. It is not that General Motors, or any company, does not think in terms of lots of goals. The question is whether they see goals other than money as intermediate goals, with the sole ultimate goal being profit, or whether they see them as a set of incommensurable goals. German companies speak of social goals and profit goals and judgements to be made as to the trade-off. I have spoken to lots of businessmen about this corporate social responsibility area, and a key reason they do not like it is that they feel uncomfortable about having to justify a judgement if there is more than one yardstick. If there is one yardstick, that makes it easy for a chairman to say, 'I did this corporate social responsibility thing because it will boost profits'. But if you cannot prove it will boost profits then it is much more difficult for them. There is a need to get back to making difficult judgements about trade-offs, rather than assuming it is all commensurable.

Robert H. Frank
There are companies that do seem to care about the customer being happy, rather than just making money. I think they believe, at the same time, that if they make the customer really happy they probably will make money. Perhaps that is even the best way to make money. Apple claims to be such a company, and if you go by the hard data on customer attitudes about the products, they do seem to deliver on what they claim they are aiming at and they make an extraordinary amount of money

in the process. Talking to people who have worked there for a long time, it is clear that they do not pay top dollar, but they get people who eagerly seek positions there because they have a sense of mission. That is a very well-established pattern in the corporate world. Not every corporation tries to occupy that part of the space, but there have been conspicuous examples of ones that have done very successfully by being able to attract talent that is willing to work for less than the going rate, or is better than the going quality level, just because they have a sense of mission.

Perry Anderson
Do you think the work satisfaction of the people who are actually producing their machines in Foxconn, in Fujian, is so great?

Robert H. Frank
As far as we know, it is much higher than the competition's satisfaction.

Steven Lukes
I just want to add something to what you said, Bob. I have just read a book by a young colleague of mine, Gabriel Abend, which is a history of business ethics.[6] What John was describing – the ethical economy, the embedded economy – has been the staple of teaching in business schools for over a century. The idea of characterising capitalist business as naked self-interest – some kinds of economists do this, but surely in the corporate world itself it is the opposite?

John Milbank
That was part of what I was saying. To some extent, we are less capitalist than the economic books say. I was also probing the issue of whether, if you pursue social benefit and social value ultimately for utilitarian profit-orientated

reasons, it will not happen. It will be muted and it will be corrupted. Curiously, you will also lose some economic benefit by not being sincere. As I read the Harvard Business School arguments, they are arguing in a very utilitarian way, not a virtue ethic way. I think you can go beyond that.

Steven Lukes
No, but Bob Frank's point is that this is not just window-dressing. Insofar as this is actually instilled as a belief, then it works.

John Milbank
Great, but it is still too marginal. Let us make it more central.

Robert Skidelsky
All right, it works in the sense that it makes the consumer happy, but what value does one attach to false belief? One can be deluded and happy. In other words, to make someone happy is certainly admirable, but then you also want to ask, 'Are they right to be happy in this situation?' When confronted with an absolutely shoddy product with brilliant advertising behind it, they then say 'We are satisfied with this.' Is that a good state of mind for them to be in?

Felix Martin
Obviously it is true that they teach business ethics; it is true that John Lewis exists; it is true that on the level of retail trading or newsagents, people are not rabid capitalists thinking only of their self-interest. It is true that we economists are completely nuts and that most of our microeconomic models for years treated people like that and so on. Nevertheless, there is a reason why we are sitting here discussing this, which is that in reality, in a monetary economy, all of this stuff is completely

dominant. It works outwards from the brain of the system, where I work – in the financial markets, the money markets and the bond markets. It is pure oxygen. There is obviously no room for sympathy in those markets, in the way they are structured and set up. They are purely numerical. It is purely abstract. This goes down all the way through the banking system to coordinate economic activity. Right down at the bottom, of course, it is true that sympathy creeps in. The fact that it is contradictory to what we do – I agree with you, Geoffrey – does not mean that it is any less true.

Showkat Ali
This is a question about Edward's talk. You claimed that sex has an inherent goal – a telos – which you tried to clarify in your three features of sex. Now, if we grant those assumptions then it seems clear that commercial sex does not meet those requirements, but it also seems that there are instances of non-commercial sex that might not meet them either.

Edward Skidelsky
I agree. There are other forms of sexual perversion aside from prostitution.

Showkat Ali
Should that not fit uncomfortably with your point about sex having an inherent goal?

Glen Newey
Can I come in on that? Given the Aristotelian tenor of a lot of the remarks – and I do not know how far you would go – it seemed to me quite strange to characterise the eternal aim of sex in that way. You have the heterosexual couple who decide that they are going to procreate, and they think, 'Oh, I don't really fancy it, but we're going to go through the deed.' Does that count as an example of corrupting sex?

Edward Skidelsky
Yes, I think so. Perhaps you know the film *The Big Lebowski* – it is a very good film. There is a scene in which a couple have sex, and then she immediately starts rolling back and rocking around. He says, 'What are you doing?' She says, 'I'm trying to get pregnant, of course. Why do you think I slept with you?' That is as repulsive, in a way, as paying for sex.

Glen Newey
I think we have come quite a long way from Aristotle to say that.

Edward Skidelsky
I am not wedded to every single Aristotelian doctrine.

John Milbank
You can be more Aristotelian than Aristotle.

Nan Craig
I was thinking of another example. I know you threw out the idea of therapeutic sexual prostitutes, but I have seen mention recently of groups of sex workers who provide sexual services for people with really severe disabilities, who have not been able to find anyone else to have sex with, or for whom sex is physically difficult. Those people, apart from doing it for the money, seem to be doing it for other reasons. Clearly, that undermines the telos of sex as you described it. If, for instance, they were doing that work *pro bono*, would that still be corrupting?

John Milbank
I think it is still corrupt.

Edward Skidelsky
Well, I defer to the theologian here.

John Milbank
Yes, I think so, because it is not sex.

Nan Craig
But it is not the money that is corrupting it, then.

John Milbank
It is using sex to be charitable, and that is neither charity nor sex.

Notes

1. Michael Sandel, *What Money Can't Buy* (London: Allen Lane, 2012).
2. Giorgio Agamben, *Homo Sacer: Sovereign Power and Bare Life*, tr. Daniel Heller-Roazen (Stanford: Stanford University Press, 1998).
3. Jean-Claude Michéa, *The Realm of Lesser Evil: An Essay on Liberal Civilisation*, tr. David Fernbach (Cambridge: Polity, 2009).
4. Luigino Bruni and Stefano Zamagni, *Civil Economy: Efficiency, Equity and Public Happiness* (Bern: Peter Lang, 2007).
5. J.M. Keynes quoted in Virginia Woolf, *The Diary of Virginia Woolf, Volume IV*, entry for 19 April 1934, ed. Ann Olivier Bell (London: Hogarth Press, 1982).
6. Gabriel Abend, *The Moral Background: An Inquiry into the History of Business Ethics* (Princeton: Princeton University Press, 2014).

Session 4

The Meaning of Money

Felix Martin

Actually, I hesitate to start on this topic of the meaning of money, because not only am I here with all of you, who are real experts, much more expert than I am and proper scholars, and I am basically just a bit of a yahoo, a practitioner in the world of money – I run a bond fund – but also because I am aware that in no other field than money is there a greater risk of being dismissed as a complete crank when you claim to have discovered the meaning of it. I am sure many of you will know Paul Samuelson, the great Nobel Prize-winning American economist. He used to say, 'not one man in 10,000 understands the monetary question, and you meet him every day'. So here am I, and you have just met me.

What is a dollar? What actually is a euro, a pound, or yen? Not, of course, a dollar note, or a euro coin, or a pound coin, but the dollar, the euro, the pound itself. Well, as Alfred Mitchell Innes, the great but neglected monetary scholar of the 20th century said, 'the hand has never touched, nor the eye seen, a dollar'. That, of course, is true, because a pound, a dollar, a yen, a euro, they are just units of measurement of an abstract scale of value. It is very easy to think, of course, that they are something physical, and many people have thought like that over the years, particularly in times when we had forms of currency that were made of precious metal and therefore had some intrinsic value of their own. It is more difficult to think of that when we really consider it these days, when most money is electronic, when most money is composed of the liabilities of banks, and yet we do still have the habit of thinking like that.

However, it is this feature – the monetary unit – which distinguishes, I think, economic value from all these other scales of value that we have been talking about here today, these incommensurable scales, more modest scales of value that do not try and apply themselves to absolutely everything in the world as the scale of economic value does: sentimental value, religious value, honorific value, aesthetic value, and so on and so forth. The thing which distinguishes monetary or economic value is that it has an explicit standard; a standard unit. But what is this standard? Where does it come from, and what exactly does it mean? These, I have always thought, ever since I started studying economics, which is my subject, should surely be the absolutely canonical and central questions of money and monetary economics, and yet the strange thing is that they appear almost nowhere in economic consideration of money. Standard classical economics, I am sure you are all aware, talks about money as a unit of account, a medium of exchange and a store of value, but most economic inquiry has focused on its role as a medium of exchange and a store of value, and not on its role as a unit of account, where this unit comes from and what it means. That is what our session is discussing this evening.

In order to make a small contribution for you, I thought I would tell you a story. It is a story that I was going to put into *Money: The Unauthorised Biography* but it got left out in the end, so I will tell you it anyway, because it has illuminated the way that I have been able to answer this question; and it begins in the 1920s in Cambridge, the Bloomsbury era, in honour of Robert.

The story begins with two figures that some of you will be familiar with: C. K. Ogden, the great polymath of the day, and his friend, I. A. Richards, who was to become an eminent literary critic. These two men had an ingenious idea, which was a radical reform of the English language, to make it simple and clear enough to be learned and used internationally. If English grammar, vocabulary and syntax could be dramatically simplified and made to follow a small number of logical rules, the meaning of words would cease to be a cause of confusion and become instead a framework for objective thought and a spur to rational action. This new simplified language would eliminate once and for all the obfuscation and misunderstanding that was the root cause of nationalistic small-mindedness and the chief playground of the warmongering demagogues.

They christened their solution 'Basic English', and published its manifesto, along with its proposed vocabulary of only 850 words – including a mere 18 verbs – in January, 1929.[1] 'All that remains', wrote Ogden and Richards, 'is to satisfy the sceptic who finds it impossible to believe that with so few words anything approaching a passable English idiom can be achieved.'[2] The two evangelists were not found wanting in this respect. Their indefatigable efforts to promote the new system found a ready audience with populations sickened by two decades of international strife: Basic English rapidly caught on. An orthological institute was established in Cambridge and charged with spreading the system round the world: by 1935 it had representatives in 35 countries, from Turkey to the Soviet Union, and from Siam to Mexico.[3] As the world lurched towards another world war in the late 1930s, the Basic English movement achieved ever more widespread popularity and support. In 1939, three American foundations paid for 200 teachers to visit Cambridge to learn the universal language that might yet save the world. By the autumn of 1939, there were no fewer than 8,000 applicants for a session in Basic English at the British Council in Athens.

And then, on 6 September 1943, in the midst of the war, Basic English achieved what looked like its apotheosis: the British Prime Minister Winston Churchill, speaking on the occasion of an award of an honorary degree from Harvard, identified Basic English as a bright prospect for the post-war world order. He called it 'the head-stream of what might well be a mighty fertilising and healthgiving river'. He predicted that 'it would be a grand convenience to us all to be able to move freely about the world and be able to find everywhere a medium, albeit primitive, of intercourse and understanding; an advantage to many races and an aid to the building up of our new structure of preserving peace'. Basic English, it seemed, was to be the wonder-weapon of the coming peace.

Unfortunately, the results of this spectacular endorsement were disastrous. There was an immediate shortage of teaching materials, because so many people wanted to study Basic English. Then the US foundations stopped funding it, because they believed that the British government was funding it – after all, it had been endorsed by Churchill. Churchill's influence indeed ensured that a War Cabinet Committee for Basic English was set up, but only years of tedious negotiations over state funding ensued. They ended in acrimony and recrimination, the Committee Secretary concluding at the end of these negotiations that, 'despite his idealistic appearance, Ogden was a very difficult man; inaccessible, violently prejudiced and with a most unexpectedly shrewd and even over-developed business sense'.

The whole thing, in the end, came to nothing, of course. Basic English is completely forgotten these days. Ogden himself very sadly ended up retiring to his club in Pall Mall, just round the corner, where a contemporary, full of pity, memorialised him as 'the life and soul of the Athenaeum'; a very sorry fate, I think. But the story of this Basic English – idealistic origins, ambitious proponents, brief moment in the sun, collapse – is a very familiar one. There have been lots of attempts throughout history by starry-eyed mavericks to reinvent or reform languages on their own, and they have all, more or less, met the same fate. Even Esperanto, of course the most well-known, is really just a plaything for cranks, and the reason for that is obvious. Language, as we all know, is a social phenomenon, and it is no good, on your own, trying to invent your own language and then thinking it is going to take off and compete with any of the already existing languages. Languages emerge from the spontaneous interaction of people in society, and even grand and well-funded institutions appointed as the guardians of linguistic purity do not really have control over them. Year after year, the *Académie Française* – the official body charged with making the French language 'pure, eloquent, and capable of treating the arts and sciences' – issues ultimatums decreeing that English words are not part of the French language. Yet men and women the length and breadth of France continue to spend *le weekend* indulging in a spot of *jogging* before tucking into *des hamburgers* to the sounds of *le rock'n'roll*.

The fact is that almost any attempt to control language is doomed to failure. And when the attempt is pioneered almost single-handedly by a quixotic ideologue operating from the depths of the Cambridgeshire fens, it becomes frighteningly reminiscent of the surreal over-confidence of Humpty-Dumpty when he boasts to Alice in Looking-Glass Land: 'When *I* use a word ... it means just what I choose it to mean – neither more nor less.'[4] On this side of the Looking-Glass, however, a word means what everyone uses it to mean – and there's no point in Humpty-Dumpty or anyone else unilaterally deciding otherwise.

At least, that seems to be the rule when it comes to eccentric individuals and pedantic quangos. The 20th century provided ample evidence that there is however one kind of institution that can be really rather effective at manipulating the meaning of language: the totalitarian state. During the early decades of Soviet rule in Russia, orthodox theory held that language as we know it – along with the state, and indeed money – would wither away as true socialism was gradually achieved. The Soviet linguistic scholar N. J. Marr foresaw a future in which, as one expert puts it, 'the workers would give up speech – the formal and reactionary medium bequeathed to them by the obscurantist past – and communicate directly, by pure thought alone'.[5] In the event, language left to its own devices proved frustratingly resilient – and just as was the case with money and the state, the Party quickly realised therefore that what was not going to disappear must instead be press-ganged into the total service of Soviet ideology. There was already a robust tradition in Russia of so-called 'wooden language' – the impenetrable idiom of the Tsarist bureaucracy, designed to exclude and baffle the general public, and in doing so impress upon them the power beyond question of the state and its administrative elite.[6] Over the course of the 20th century, the Soviet Communist Party and its imitators around the world would bring this model of turning language into a brutal political tool to its highest – or perhaps one should say lowest – perfection.

The result was the totalitarian language of Soviet Communism darkly parodied by George Orwell as 'Newspeak' in his dystopian novel *1984*.[7] Through its domination of the media and the oppressive wordiness of its culture, the Soviet regime set about deploying language as its chief tool for ideological brain-washing. 'How have we changed the Russian language?' asked Josef Stalin rhetorically. 'A great many old words are no longer part of its vocabulary: the semantic meaning of a great many others has been changed: we have improved the grammatical structure of the language.'[8] He was referring to the development of the new idiom deployed relentlessly by the Party in all its communications with the people: the incessant resort to martial vocabulary, even in the most innocuous of contexts (one infamous example saw a Czech Party official vowing to 'batter the warmongers to death with peace'); the fondness for abstract nouns whose meaning could change with changing policy (one scholar lists 81 different 'isms', from neutralism to deviationism and practicism to theoreticism, often found in official journalism and speeches – and these were only the most commonly used ones); the constant reference to 'We', which had ceased to mean 'me and you' and now only meant 'you'; the blanket use of impersonal and passive phrasing to impress the determination of events by objective, historical forces; and so on.[9]

Outside observers like Orwell objected that, however effective this distorted, ideological language was at closing down people's mental universes, obliterating the possibility for non-political conversation, and strengthening the power of the Party, it was not in fact an exercise in improving language, but in destroying it as a means of free and humane communication. Rather than changing the meaning of words, totalitarian language really just made words meaningless – and transformed them into a tool, the single purpose of which was to impress the power of the Party on its subjects. The appalling depths plumbed by the official Soviet style demonstrates the lighter side of Orwell's point. Who, after all, could really take seriously the garbled imagery of 'the fascist octopus has sung his swan song' or 'the jackboot is thrown into the melting pot'?[10] And the purpose of the immortal pronouncement that 'having thrown away the fig-leaf of neo-colonialism, imperialism at last reveals its true face', could hardly lie in its meaning.[11] It is, however, the chilling way totalitarian language was used to promote terror that seals his case. The slogan over the main gate at Auschwitz alleged that 'work makes you free'. Solzhenitsyn reported a sign in a Soviet gulag that exhorted the starving inmates to 'let a surge of the competitive spirit give the lie to the new slanders of the capitalists about forced labour in the USSR'.[12] From the perspective of their authors, the flagrant perversion of reality that such sickening statements represented was not, as it might naturally seem to a Western audience, a flaw – quite the opposite. As the French Sovietologist Françoise Thom has explained, 'these slogans are not intended to persuade the prisoner how fortunate he is: on the contrary, their purpose is to remind him that there is no remedy for his abasement, that the regime feels free to treat reality with the same contempt that it treats him, and that reality, so defined, is, like himself, without redress'.[13] The literal meaning of the words has ceased to be of any importance at all – they have become a mere expression of power. 'Far from being a mark of weakness, these incredible lies … advertise the absolute hold which totalitarian regimes have on their subjects.'[14]

We must, therefore, modify our earlier conclusion regarding the susceptibility of language to deliberate control. Eccentric individuals might not be able to control the meaning of words. The state, however, is potentially a different matter. It is in a position to dominate the airwaves – so it can achieve a level of influence that the individual cannot. Even more importantly, it can set the terms on which its citizens communicate with it – and since most citizens rely on the state for something, their language can be made to fit in. The state, therefore, can control language and its meaning – even if only, as Orwell pointed out, to destroy it as a means of genuine conversation.

But this conclusion too is not quite correct. The annals of the 20th century are depressingly full of the dismal linguistic records of totalitarian states. They also contain, however, inspiring stories of those who devised ways to defy them. Orwell's *1984* is a fictional version of just such an attempt. The book's hero, Winston Smith, first realises the possibility of escape from the false reality which the Party has created with its Newspeak when he overhears a working-class woman singing an old English nursery song – 'Oranges and Lemons' – whilst hanging out her washing. The unexpected departure from the deadening and meaningless wooden language of the state provides Smith with the crucial reminder that there is a world beyond the Party's ideology in which people communicate with one another using a germane vernacular, rather than simply demonstrating their loyalty to the Party line by repeating set phrases that have lost all literal meaning.

It is, however, the diary of a great linguistic expert who became trapped under the tyranny of Nazi Germany that provides the most famous blueprint for how to escape totalitarian language in the real world of the 20th century. Viktor Klemperer was a professor of philology in Dresden before World War II, and a Jew. With the ascent to power of the Nazis he found his academic activities ever more strictly curtailed – although the classification of his wife as an Aryan saved him from the worst persecution for some time. Ultimately, he was expelled from his post and placed under house arrest, from which he would have been deported to the camps had he not escaped during the chaos of the Allied bombing of Dresden in February 1945. As a philologist, Klemperer was acutely aware of the central role that language was playing in the degradation of German society. 'Nazism', he wrote, 'permeated the flesh and blood of the people through single words, idioms, and sentence structures which were imposed on them in a million repetitions and taken on board mechanically and unconsciously'.[15] At first he found his predicament, cooped up in his apartment with nothing to do but listen to a constant stream of Party propaganda on the radio, hopeless. He hated the fact that he had lost his physical freedom – but he hated even more the idea that he might, like the rest of the German-speaking world, lose his ability to think properly because of the incessant barrage of Nazi language. But then he had an idea.

The idea was to keep a detailed record of the Nazi debauching of the German language and its effect on political discourse and on everyday behaviour. People were rapidly succumbing to the thought patterns of Nazi language, so that 'by tomorrow everything will already look different, by tomorrow everything will already feel different'.[16] He would therefore keep a linguistic diary in order to 'keep hold of how things reveal themselves at this very moment and what the effects are'.[17] He christened his project 'LTI' – an abbreviation of the Latin title 'Lingua Tertii Imperii' ('The Language of the Third Reich'). The very title itself was an act of resistance – pillorying the Nazi fondness for deploying foreign phraseology in order to lend fake cachet to its nomenclature, and its proclivity for abbreviations in order to exclude those unfamiliar with the jargon.[18] 'LTI', Klemperer wrote, 'appears first in my diary as a playful little piece of parody, almost immediately afterwards as a laconic *aide-memoire* … and then very soon, and for the duration of those terrible years, as an act of self-defence, an SOS to myself'.[19] Klemperer had discovered a priceless instrument of dissent in a totalitarian society – a means of keeping hold of objective reality in defiance of the ideological brain-washing of the Party and its language. 'Many a time I have been reminded of an old Berlin anecdote', he wrote. '"Father," a young boy asks in the circus, "What is the man up there on the tightrope doing with that pole?" – "Silly boy, it's a balancing pole, and it's what's holding him steady." – "Oh dear, father, what if he lets go of it?" – "Silly boy, he's holding it steady of course!" Again and again during these years my diary was my balancing pole, without which I would have fallen down a hundred times.'[20]

What Orwell's *1984* suggested in fiction, and Klemperer's *LTI* proved in real life, is that the state's control of language can never be absolute. Certainly, a totalitarian state can manipulate meaning, bastardise syntax and turn an ancient and living language into a zombified slave of political power – things that individual effort can never achieve, as the adventure of Basic English showed. But push things beyond a certain point, and the everyday users of that language will rebel. Language is a social phenomenon. Real social life will always be richer by far than the limited imaginations of Party ideologues – consisting as it does of the genuine human wealth of family and friendship rather than Olympian abstractions like class struggle and racial purity. Vernacular language will always find a way to hold its conversations on these most humane of topics – to break the bounds in which a totalitarian state attempts to shackle it once they become too oppressively tight.

What is the point of this story about language: the impossibility of inventing it on your own; the potential of the state to manipulate it, but the way that people can get round that manipulation, if it becomes too extreme? Well, because I think the monetary standard – which is a very elusive topic, especially to us economists, because we are trained not to think about it – is a very, very good and close analogy.

First, the monetary standard is intrinsically social. You cannot invent it on your own. A famous economist once said – I cannot remember who it is, but Robert Frank might be able to remember – but one of these famous neoclassical economists once said, 'anyone can issue their own money. The problem is getting it accepted'. And that is not quite right. I mean, it is true that anyone can write IOUs, and – depending on how other people rate your creditworthiness and the liquidity of these IOUs – they could circulate as money. Anyone can do that. That is just a private money. There are lots of those, but this famous economist was making an important prior assumption: that these IOUs are denominated in dollars or euros or pounds or something – an existing unit of account. Because what no one can do is issue their own money, regardless of how creditworthy in issue they are, *denominated in their own private monetary unit.* It would be quite literally meaningless. No one would understand what they meant.

Second, the state is not like you and me, however. It is very large and very influential; almost everyone has to deal with it regularly, and it can to an extent dictate terms. So the state – especially a totalitarian state – can mess around with the meaning of words. And when it comes to the monetary standard, the creditworthiness and liquidity of the sovereign's promises to pay do have a very significant effect on the value of the monetary standard and the extent to which the general public use it to denominate private assessments of economic value. That is why hyperinflations are so invariably associated with the collapse of sovereign credit and the legitimacy of the state itself.

However, third, the state's control of the monetary standard is not absolute. If the monetary standard, like a totalitarian language, becomes so detached from reality as to be useless in the eyes of its private users, society can and will improvise an alternative. That's why

The Meaning of Money 115

when inflation gets out of control, for example, people start to redenominate prices in dollars or euros – hard currency – even though there might be no dollars or euros actually in circulation. That is quite a common thing to happen. There are historical examples – such as Italian exchange bankers during the 16th century, or much more recently in Argentina after their crisis – of coming up with a new standard all of their own. Anyway, in either case they find themselves a monetary standard that will actually serve its stated purpose, which is the coordination of monetary society, to replace the one that the state has rendered senseless.

What was the point of asking this question as to the meaning of money, and why have I said all this about the monetary standard? It is because if you believe that there are problems with monetary society – that it is prone to excess and wasteful competition (that was a subject that Robert Frank dealt with in the first session); that it produces inequality; that it is prone to debt crises (when you have fixed nominal contracts with varying expectations, you always end up with these debt crises) – then we are bound to ask: How should we resolve these problems of monetary society?

We have heard several answers already today. We heard – although I may be putting words into Robert Skidelsky's mouth – about a solution which is to say, 'well, we should reduce the scope of monetary society. We should reduce the extent to which money is the coordinating mechanism. We should canalise or repress money in some way.' We heard about what we were discussing in the last session: John Milbank was describing various sorts of micro-reforms, legal reforms, ways of trying to either change people's minds and their objectives or to try to capture them in a web of legislation which makes them do things more sensibly, but not fundamentally changing money itself. We heard from Robert Frank a very persuasive argument about fiscal measures, tax and expenditure, and how that could improve things. Again, not changing money itself but trying to use fiscal measures outside that to make the outcomes of monetary society better.

I want to suggest that there is one very obvious tool and lever – this is what I am going to end with – that we have not discussed yet. If you think money is deficient in these respects, there is a problem, because we are stuck with it. It is not going to go away. On the other hand, if money is a social technology, there is an opportunity, because you can do something with money itself, not with stuff outside money: fiscal measures, legal measures and so on. You can do these as well, they are not mutually exclusive, obviously, but there is one obvious and very effective lever available to tackle these ills, and it is nothing other than the manipulation of the monetary standard itself by a democratic sovereign under the rule of law.

What I am talking about I think has a lot of relevance to our time right now. We are living with a huge overhang of debt, which is constraining the economy, which is the expression in many countries, in Western Europe, of a great inequality between age groups and between rich and poor people. There is something, a single thing, a very simple thing to do, which we could do to correct these ills. It is not exclusive, as I said, of all these other things that we have been talking about. It is, of course, to aim for some years of inflation so that we can have a situation like we had in the 1970s here in the UK. That was a decade during which my retired grandfather living off his pension was impoverished, while my young parents were able to buy a great big house. My parents were terribly worried about their mortgage at the beginning of the decade – but by the end of it they were not worried at all, because inflation had eroded the value of their debt. Inflation had, by the very same token, eroded the value of my grandfather's fixed pension income. That was just, of course, a huge redistribution of wealth from my grandfather's generation to my parents' generation, which I do not believe would have been achievable by any kind of fiscal or microeconomic or legal changes. Yet it was done with one pull of a single lever.

Geoffrey Hosking

There is one element here which I want to emphasise and put right at the centre of the argument, and that is, of course, trust. When I talk about trust, I am not talking so much about personal trust, trust between individuals. I do not exclude it altogether, but I am talking more about social trust – that is really to say the social framework within which personal trust takes place, but also trust in institutions and processes, so I am not just talking about personal trust. My basic thesis is that trust in society, social trust, is mediated through symbolic systems and the associated institutions. In my book[21] I have considered briefly some of them: law, science and various forms of culture, for example, and the institutions which go with those, but the two principal symbolic systems which I am writing about are religion and money. Obviously I am going to concentrate on money here.

I call money a symbol of trust, and I will explain why. Consider what happens nowadays when you hire a car. You show your driving licence, you make a down-payment, and that payment includes third-party insurance and probably a deposit of several hundred pounds in case you damage the car seriously, or it is stolen. You then mark a diagram which indicates existing damage and then you drive away. Now, think about what happens there. The hire firm entrusts you with a vehicle worth several thousand pounds, easily damaged and capable of killing someone if you misuse it. At the same time, you trust the hire company to have serviced the car properly so that it will not malfunction, since if it does you yourself might well be killed or seriously injured. You and the firm know very little about each other. Not perhaps nothing; if the firm had a very bad reputation you might know about that, but basically you and the firm know very little about each other. But you trust each other with resources of very considerable importance, and this is merely a routine example of what I call 'strong thin trust'.

I have explained that term in the book. Briefly, what I mean by that is that thick trust is trust in somebody you know well, or an institution you know well, have a lot of experience of. Thin trust is trust in somebody you do not know well. Strong trust is trust where you entrust serious resources, like your life or your health or your old age. Weak trust is when you are not really dealing with very serious resources. Strong thin trust, then, is entrusting considerable resources to a person or institution you know little about. It sounds foolhardy, but it happens all the time in the modern world.

What is it that lubricates this strong thin trust which, I have argued in my book, is characteristic of modern society? Actually, we often misunderstand the nature of trust because we do not think of thin trust as trust. That is quite a problem; I may come back to it. What lubricates this exchange of trust? The central feature is money. There are, as I say, other aspects involved, but this is the central feature. This transaction would be totally impossible without money. I mean, instead of money, what would

I offer the car hire firm – a paper on the emancipation of the serfs in 19th-century Russia? I cannot imagine that a car hire firm would find much use for that, so money is absolutely crucial, and since this kind of mutual trust – semi-conscious, unconscious – is so common in everyday life, we scarcely notice it.

Another central argument which I make about trust is that the human predisposition to trust is very strong indeed. Now, you may doubt that; it sounds, in a way, a bit idealistic, but my studies have convinced me that that is the case. The most perceptive writer on money is the German philosopher and sociologist, Georg Simmel, and he is also in many ways the most perceptive writer on trust and the way it operates in society. Simmel came to the conclusion that money embodies a generalised social trust, whose justification is not demonstrable, but without which any social or economic life is inconceivable. Just to quote him briefly: 'without the general trust that people have in each other, society itself would disintegrate, for very few relationships are based entirely upon what is known with certainty about another person, and very few relationships would endure if trust were not as strong as, or stronger than, rational proof or personal observation'.[22]

Now, my contention is that the function of money is to fix that human predisposition to trust and make it effective economically. One can imagine a life without money. Indeed, for some socialists, as you know, that was an ideal. It is possible to exchange goods and services either through barter or through reciprocal gifts, but so cumbersome are both that from the time of the very earliest records societies were devising objects that could be used as a generally applicable standard of value and to enable more diverse forms of exchange. I do not think of this as premonetary, but we have had an argument about that already. It is certainly precoinage. All societies beyond the very primitive have felt the need to create symbols they could trust as means of exchange and stable indicators of value, since exchange, sale or purchase all involve some risk.

If you go to the Ashmolean exhibition in Oxford, it has a permanent exhibition of the different types of money which have been used over the centuries – indeed, millennia. It includes shells, bangles, stones, rolls of cloth, various metals, and paper; objects that appear to have nothing in common except that, as the exhibition leaflet states, they all work as money because people place trust in them when they are used in transactions. Now, I was going to quote Homer here, but I do this with some trepidation. In Homer, cattle actually fulfil this role. Our word 'pecuniary' is derived from the Latin *pecus*, meaning 'cattle', but cattle is jolly inconvenient as a unit of value, because it comes in bulky, rather highvalue units. It was handier to use something smaller, more portable and more flexible. Cowrie shells were popular in many societies, being light, not too easy to find and valuable of themselves since they could be worn as ornaments, and I understand – although I cannot vouch for this – that the Chinese pictogram for money still contains the root image of the cowrie shell.

Obviously, metal coins had considerable advantages, once they began to be used. They were in themselves valuable. That is quite important, since gold, silver and copper were found in limited supply and had first to be mined and refined. They could be manufactured in different weights to denote different values, and they could be carried in the hand, pouch or pocket. Now, another important element comes in here. Money will be more trusted if it bears the symbolism of an authoritative institution widely trusted in the community. Coinage, I think, bears witness to that. The coins of the ancient Greek city of Lydia bore the image of a lion's head, which was the city's emblem. Similarly, Corinthian coins had a winged horse and Athenian ones an owl. Roman Republican coins bore the image of Juno, goddess of the mint, or of mythological heroes. In Imperial Rome, of course, the head of the emperor validated a coin. In the Abbasid Caliphate, coins bore the motto 'There is no God but God', indicating the way in which religion and money actually are quite closely related, and of course the modern US dollar declares, 'In God We Trust.'

This is an important point: money is more trusted when it is issued and guaranteed by a sovereign authority known to be powerful, able to enforce its rule. So strong is the association of money with power that in his recent history of finance Niall Ferguson called money 'portable power'.[23] In another passage of the book he also calls it 'trust inscribed'. Now, both tend to go together, as I have just suggested, but in my view trust is more important than power. Money that is not trusted, as in times of hyperinflation, has little or no power. The German hyperinflation of 1922 to 1923 offers a terrible example of this. At its height, a lifetime's savings would buy no more than a cup of coffee. A contemporary witness recalled: 'dentists and doctors stopped charging in currency and demanded butter or eggs', but the farmers, of course, were holding back their produce. A Bavarian farmer is quoted as saying, 'we don't want any Jew confetti from Berlin'. The flight from currency that began with the buying of diamonds, gold, country houses and antiques now extended to minor and almost useless items. The law-abiding country crumpled into petty thievery. Copper pipes and brass armatures were not safe; gasoline was siphoned from cars. People bought things they did not need and used them to barter: a pair of shoes for a shirt, some crockery for coffee. Berlin had a 'witches' Sabbath atmosphere'.

The reference to Jews and witches here reminds one that what is involved is intense distrust, which needs to attract itself to an object. Money, when it is not a mediator of trust, becomes a powerful mediator of distrust, and this is part of the downside of money, which I am going to talk about more towards the end. Elias Canetti, and not only he, thought that the inflation was decisive in turning many Germans towards anti-Semitism, because of Jews' long-standing connection with money, their skill in speculation, the way they flocked together in money markets and so on. He has quite a long section on this.

Money illustrates what I have come to see as a general rule of trust. We all tend to trust beyond the point at which rational reflection would suggest we ought not to trust any longer, but once a tipping point has been reached we move to distrust abruptly and cumulatively. The human predisposition to trust is very strong, but it is not infinite, and when it comes to an end distrust swings in very sharply. This is basically why unregulated markets generate booms and busts which dislocate entire economies. Trust is highly contagious. During a boom, investors pile aboard the gravy train, not wanting to be left out or outdone by rivals, and this carries on well beyond the point at which rational consideration ought to prevail. But then some event, or even just a rumour, casts doubt on the long-term prospects. One or two major investors calculate that the commodity or the share price no longer matches the risk, and they begin to sell. News spreads that something is wrong. Distrust sets in and is equally contagious. Panic, in fact, begins, and feeds on itself. The price plunges. Investors sell out hastily without even pausing to make fuller enquiry, lest delay lose them even more money. Those who borrowed heavily to buy on the upswing are ruined; firms go bankrupt, and even banks may collapse. Exaggerated trust turns to equally exaggerated and destructive distrust.

Money embodies all the generic features of trust and distrust, but there is another problem, too, about money. We have been talking about this partly today. It is nicely illustrated by two paintings that hang side by side in the Bruges Art Gallery in Belgium. The paintings are by Jan Provoost. One of them shows a miserly merchant on his deathbed, pointing to the substantial positive balance in his ledger and desperately trying to pass a promissory note across to the next painting, which is obviously the afterlife. There, a grinning skeleton refuses to accept it and preaches a little sermon on the limitations of money. A reverend gentleman in the background appears to corroborate the skeleton's sentiments. Money has no power in the afterlife; money has no power in eternity. Provoost's painting points to a salient and disturbing feature of money as a symbolic system: its disconnection from eternal values, and, I would say, its disconnection from other trust-generating symbolic systems. Most symbolic systems create meanings which combine with each other to generate further meanings. This is how advances are made in, for example, mathematics and the sciences, through reflecting on how we interpret what we already understand and then linking it with other aspects of that symbolic system, or other symbolic systems.

Money, however, is strangely impoverished and isolationist in this respect. It can beget a bewildering variety of practices and financial institutions, but no meanings which refer to other symbolic systems. It is like an inert element which does not combine with other chemical substances. Money is the purest example of the tool, being highly versatile, applicable to almost any use. It is neutral, precisely calculable and infinitely fungible, and it tends to reduce all our experience to a series of quantitatively conceived means, without ends and without autonomous significance. In that way, when detached from the objects it enables us to exchange, it actually tends to drain other symbolic systems of their significance. In the words of Georg Simmel, 'money is everywhere conceived as purpose, and countless things which are really ends in themselves are thereby degraded to mere means'. Or in the more elegant words of Oscar Wilde, it encourages those people who 'know the price of everything and the value of nothing'.

Indeed, it may be worse than that. When money completely detaches itself from other symbolic systems, it can become extremely dangerous. It metastasises and takes control over them, implanting in them cancerous cells of its own value-neutrality. Those engaged in the business of money tend to assume that they are emancipated from ethics, from religion, and – whenever they can manage it – even from law. When they operate in the global economy, they also disdain the state as a public risk manager. That is another of my themes in the book, that a state is a public risk manager, and therefore in some kind of way offers the underpinning of a generalised social trust. This, of course, is what Karl Marx was referring to when he wrote, 'the bourgeoisie, wherever it has got the upper hand, has put an end to all feudal, patriarchal idyllic relations ... and has left remaining no other nexus between man and man than naked self-interest, than callous cash payment'. And this is why the Catholic Church in the past and Islam in the present day banned usury. In one passage of his *Philosophy of Money*, Simmel compares the power of money to the power of God: 'insofar as money becomes the absolutely sufficient expression and equivalent of all values, it rises to abstract heights way above the whole broad diversity of objects. It becomes the centre in which the most opposed, the most estranged and the most distant things find their common denominator and come into contact with one another'.

We have already had examples of money's incursion into areas of life where it seems incongruous and weakens moral standards. Devotion to money as an instrument for gaining power and ensuring security has the potential to subvert other symbolic systems. So, money is a deeply ambivalent symbolic system, a deeply ambivalent tool. It has the power to link people together in transactions and ventures which have great potential and which otherwise would not take place, but it also possesses dangerous powers which can undermine, colonise and degrade what in life we would otherwise cherish. In brief, money itself is a very serious subject. We tend to take it for granted, but its power to create and destroy social trust is right at the centre of our social and economic life, and it is important that we conceptualise it as a question of trust in the trustworthy, because that is the essential. That is the centre around which everything else moves, in my opinion, and unless we conceptualise it that way, we will not really be able to get to the heart of the problem of money.

David Graeber

I want to talk about money as a moral technology. One of the things that really fascinated me when I was working on my book on debt was the tendency of the logic of the market to colonise and invade other forms of morality, even the language of religion. Almost all the great world religions are incredibly rich in the language of finance – think about words like redemption – and this happens not just in Christianity but pretty much everywhere.

Morality tended to be treated as a matter of paying one's debts. This was one reason that I actually entered into this particular intellectual journey; I was fascinated with the moral power of the idea of debt, and its tendency to trump any other form of morality, so that people can justify things which they would never dream of trying to justify in other circumstances: the starvation and death of babies, for example, on the grounds that 'the country took out a loan'.

The invasion of the language of morality by the language of debt and money seems to be part and parcel of another phenomenon, which is the reduction of all social relations to forms of exchange. You find that almost all the great world religions begin with the premise that morality is simply a matter of paying one's debts. In Brahmin theology for example, all forms of morality are basically forms of debt. It starts with the debt to the gods, which is a debt of life, on which one pays the interest in the form of sacrifice, and will eventually pay the principal when one dies.

If one looks closely, though, the other examples that Brahmins use completely subvert the idea that these moral obligations really are debts. They say you have a debt to your parents that you will pay by having children; you also have a debt to a sage that you will pay by learning wisdom and becoming a sage. You also have a debt to humanity as a whole for making your life possible, which you will pay by being generous to strangers. None of these take the form of repaying debt in the classical sense. Ultimately, what they all seem to imply is that one erases the debt by realising that you owe all this to a totality which includes you, so the idea of debt becomes meaningless. Your debt to the gods is in fact a debt to the universe itself. You cannot really pay a debt to the universe, because that would imply that you and the universe are equal partners doing a business deal; that is, you and everything else that ever existed, including yourself, are making the deal. It is the absurdity of that which annihilates the idea of debt. In the Judaeo-Christian tradition there is a similar notion of primordial debt, but in fact it turns out that what is sacred is not paying one's debts but the cancellation of debts: redemption. It is almost as if everyone has to start out by saying, 'morality is really just paying one's debts', and then they move away from it.

The question is: Why do they have to do that? Why is it that popular conceptions of morality are already framed so deeply in debt that they always seem to have to start with those premises, even though they then inevitably move away? The best answer I could come up with is that it has to do with relations of power. Essentially, the one thing that history reveals over and over again is that a morality of debt is the most powerful way to make relations of arbitrary, violent power not only seem moral but to cast the victim in the role of the sinner, the person to blame. Mafiosi understand that, of course; so do heads of conquering armies, who generally announce that everyone owes them their lives because they have the power to kill them. It puts you in the position where you can be the benevolent person and the victims are running round, scrambling, feeling miserable and inadequate. It tends to be quite effective for a while. The problem is that it periodically explodes. As Moses Finley pointed out, there seems to be one revolutionary programme in all of antiquity, which is cancel the debts and redistribute the land, in that order.

Debt seems to inspire people to rebel more than any other form of inequality, perhaps because it is premised on an initial notion of equality. If you are saying that you are lower caste you are saying that you are fundamentally inferior, which presumably people do not like, but accept as part of the natural order of things. But if you recast this in a language of debt, you are essentially saying, 'we should have been equals, but you messed up somehow'. It seems to rankle a lot more, and the common response – which you encounter over and over again in history – is to say, 'well, wait a minute: who owes what to whom here? We make your food'.

However it is framed, what tends to happen is the only way to resist this language of debt as morality is to cast your response in that same language, in a way that actually expands the zone to which that debt applies. It causes you to reformulate moral relations in the same language. You see the same thing happening nowadays in debates over third-world debt. Who owes what to whom? That is exactly what people end up saying: 'you owe us for colonialism'; before you know it, this applies to all sorts of historical wrongs, zones that you never thought to commoditise, like ecological damage. The rebellion against debt becomes incorporated in the language of debt. With that language of debt, of course, comes the logic of exchange: that everything, essentially, can be framed in market terms.

This relation of money, debt and morality changes regularly over time, depending on the dominant conception of money, which itself depends on the dominant money form that people use in a given historical period. It seems that there are quite regular shifts across Eurasia, at least, between what I would call periods of virtual credit money and periods of commodity money, where most people are actually using some form of object, usually gold and silver, in everyday transactions, and people conceive money to be a thing. I was fascinated to discover that there is no consensus at all among economists about what money is. You would think if there was anything that economists could agree on, that would be it, but, in fact, money is a bit of a stumper for economists. The dominant schools throw their weight behind the idea of money as a medium of exchange; there are equally compelling arguments that money should be thought of as a unit of account, and therefore the tokens of money are actually tokens of debt. On this view, money is essentially circulating debt. Economists like Keith Hart argue that if you look at the two sides of a coin, you regularly see the same thing. There is one side which is a symbol of state authority, of trust and agreement, money as a social relation, which is credit; on the other side is the actual number of a unit of money, which implies that money is a commodity or a thing.

That tension is always there in the definition of money. What I would add is that, over time, the definition of money shifts back and forth. But, interestingly, virtual credit money comes first. As far as we know, if people went to the marketplace in Sumer, they certainly did not bring anything resembling cash. They certainly did not have coins; they did not even manufacture scales. They probably had the technology to do so, but they did not manufacture scales accurate enough to weigh out the tiny bits of silver that would be required to buy a pig, a sheep, a hammer, a shirt. It seems that everyday transactions were largely based on credit. Certain things did circulate in silver, for certain grains, and so on, but essentially the weight was on a credit economy, which also meant that it made it periodically possible to cancel debts, which is much harder to do in periods of commodity money. The period where money was invented, where cash currency was invented, also corresponds to what Karl Jaspers famously called the 'Axial Age', during which you also see the rise of major world philosophies and major world religions, in exactly the same place where money is first created: in the Eastern Mediterranean, in the Ganges Valley in India and the northern plains of China. It seems that coinage is invented largely as a side-effect of military technology, which is closely tied to taxation systems. Gold and silver are the sort of thing that soldiers who have been engaged in looting are most likely to be carrying around. Itinerant, heavily armed soldiers are possibly the people you would least like to extend credit to, if you are a local merchant. But they do have gold and silver. Eventually, after an initial period where money is created by merchants brokering things with soldiers, the state comes in and discovers that the easiest way to provision troops is simply to systematically give them the little bits of precious metal and then tell everyone in your country to give them back again. Suddenly you hire everyone in your kingdom to provision soldiers.

It worked brilliantly well. The fascinating thing about the Axial Age is you have standing armies; currency tends to follow standing armies. You also have the rise of world religions, which in almost every case systematically negate some of the moral logic of these impersonal cash markets which are enabled by commodity currencies, so that ideas of charity seem to always crop up simultaneously. It is as if you say, 'let us create a space where we have this thing called self-interest', and if we then simply try to get as many material things as possible for ourselves, someone else is going to come and say 'all right, well, here we will have a space where we think about why material things are not important; it is better to give than to receive'. This happens pretty much regularly in every place.

The astonishing thing is that it all coordinates really closely across Eurasia. In the Middle Ages those empires reach their apogee, and they collapse. With the disappearance of standing armies and chattel slavery, coinage largely disappears, but instead of reverting to barter, people in fact revert to credit systems. These systems of credit are essentially controlled by the moral and religious systems which originally rose in opposition to the world of cash transactions closely identified with militarism and the state which had come before. With that came the bans on usury, which did not exist in the ancient world at all. It seems that in periods where you conceive money to be a social relation, a system of social conventions – Aristotle's definition, again, was not widely adopted in antiquity but was then adopted in the Middle Ages – it becomes possible to do things like they did in the ancient world: debt cancellations in medieval Islam and Christianity, or bans on usury, which is much harder to do in periods where you consider money to be a thing.

Despite the fact that both the Athenian and the Roman constitutions were essentially created in a reaction to debt crises, ancient economies almost never resorted to full-on debt cancellations. Instead, they set up redistribution policies, where they essentially threw money at the problem, so that coinage became a sort of moral technology. For example, in ancient Athens people were actually paid to go to the agora and vote. There are all these mechanisms of redistributing money through political means, so that people did not fall so far into debt they would become slaves to the rich and thus destroy the military base of the state.

Starting in 1450, and even before the Iberian discovery of the Americas, commodity money returns in the form of bullion, and with it comes the rise once again of large empires, of standing armies, of chattel slavery, which reappears, however, in a profoundly altered form. I would argue that that period is the one that we are coming out of now, but only very slowly and haltingly. The usual cut-off point is 1971, when Nixon took the dollar definitively off the Gold Standard.

It is interesting that the ban on usury that held during the Middle Ages was gradually eroded. I have always felt that one reason why the Church was so adamantly opposed to usury as against other elements of emergent capitalism was because the morality of debt was so powerful that they could recognise a moral rival when they saw one. The fact is that debt is the most effective means to turn people into utilitarian rational actors, as economists like to imagine, where one has little choice but to see the world simply in terms of possible sources of profit and danger. One of the things I was quite fascinated with was to look at the histories of some of the people who behaved in the most bizarrely, irrationally acquisitive means you can imagine, becoming paradigms for the insatiability of human beings: the conquistadores, for example. The conquistadores were all completely in debt. They started out in debt and they never really got out of it. One reason that they were constantly looking for new kingdoms was because, even after the conquest of the Aztec kingdom, Cortez managed to get himself in debt again 15 years later and started conquering again. All the men were entirely in debt and needed to do whatever they needed to do to get gold, and so committed large atrocities to pay it back.

That kind of manipulation of debt as a form of morality in itself was unleashed and became naturalised, when you think of money as a natural thing: as an object, rather than as a social relation. As a moral technology, money allows certain types of morality to emerge which are incredibly powerful. The people in power, who originally discovered the power of the morality of debt so long ago, do not want to give them up. One of the great mysteries is when you have periods of virtual credit money, whether it is in ancient Mesopotamia or in the Middle Ages, what you normally see is people creating some means to ensure that those with the power to create credit do not effectively end up enslaving everybody else. It happens over and over again and takes different forms, hence periodic debt cancellations in ancient Mesopotamia, the famous jubilees in ancient Judea, and the various usury laws. You find that they were in combination with things like Buddhists promulgating pawn shops and other alternatives to the local loan sharks. The first prevalent use of pawn shops was actually a religious thing, by Buddhist monks in China and later, I believe, the Dominicans took it up in Europe, presumably independently.

There are all these overarching mechanisms created to protect debtors in periods of virtual credit money. Where are our versions of these mechanisms? Granted, we are only 40 years in. This is not very long by the standards we are talking of – 1,000 or 500-year cycles. But we have done exactly the opposite. What we have ended up doing is creating institutions like the IMF, or Standard & Poor's for that matter: institutions designed to protect creditors against debtors, rather than debtors against creditors. Unsurprisingly, the result for the last 40 years has been an unending series of global debt crises. Consider third-world debt, which led to surprisingly successful forms of resistance, first in East Asia, and then Latin America, from where the IMF has largely been kicked out. These debt crises are continual, they are mounting; it seems to buck the historical trend for an economy based on credit money.

This is why I emphasise the power of money as morality. I believe that there is a contradiction between the long-term interests in the system and those ideological mechanisms that would seem to be legitimating it. The morality of debt and the morality of work seem to be two areas in which the capitalist virtues, the virtues of the economic system, are deeply inculcated into popular consciousness and broadly accepted. To question that opens doors that I think a lot of people are very frightened to open, despite the fact that at this point debt cancellation is almost inevitable.

The reason I say 'almost' is because there is such resistance. It is remarkable. It is so clearly in the interests of the ruling class to start cancelling debts in a big way. The Federal Reserve has been trying really hard to get mortgage debts cancelled and they have made no headway for the last year. What is holding it back? It has to be some attachment to this fundamental moral idea, because there are not that many moral underpinnings to the system left.

One of them is the moral value of work. Keynes predicted that by now we could easily have a four-hour day, if we were so inclined, and we could remark, 'Well, obviously we are not, but obviously this shows that rather than being happy with the amount of goods we want, it has something to do with desire, it has to do with consumerism.'

I do not think that is true at all. I think that if you look at what most people do during the day, they are not doing much that contributes to the production of consumer products. In fact, an unexplored phenomenon in America today is just how many people are secretly convinced that they do not really do anything during the day: that their jobs are completely meaningless and worthless, and probably should not exist. I meet people like this all the time. I know so many people who were at their wits' end, did not know what to do, went to law school, and are now corporate lawyers. I have hardly met a single one of them who would not, at least if drunk, say, 'Actually, this job is completely stupid and should not exist.' You can make money doing this and not being a poet, or whatever they were doing before. It tells you something interesting about what we call the market that there seems to be a very limited demand for poets and talented musicians but an almost infinite demand for corporate lawyers.

I think that we have to think about this in moral terms. Think about all the people who are working four hours a day. You know, there are so many people who go into work and they sit there for eight hours but they do about three or four hours' worth of work and the rest of the time they are on Facebook or tweeting or downloading pornography or something. I talk to people and so many of them say that, 'Well, actually I do about two or three hours,' so in fact we are working fourhour days, but owing to this profound morality of labour we are not willing to actually acknowledge it.

We might want to think about the parallel with the Soviet Union. The Soviet system, I really believe, was based on a fundamental contradiction, in that they inherited an essentially anarchist constituency with a Marxist ideology. During the 1920s and 1930s, it was often noted that the difference between anarcho-syndicalist unions and socialist unions was that the anarchist unions were always asking for fewer hours, and the socialists were always asking for more money. Essentially, the socialists were those who bought into the productivist-consumerist system; anarchists just wanted out: 'We want to have nothing to do with this. We want to work as little as possible.' There was a famous debate between Marx and Bakunin over where the revolution would come: would it be the advanced industrial proletariat in Germany? Bakunin said, 'No, no, it will be the recently proletarianised peasants and artisans of Russia and Spain,' and, of course, Bakunin was right. So these anarchist constituencies who wanted fewer hours ended up creating revolutions that ended up with a Marxist-productivist elite claiming to want to create a consumer society but utterly incapable of doing so. However, one social benefit that they gave them was that you could not get fired from your job, so in fact people were working four-hour days.

The great contradiction, to me, of these systems was they could not acknowledge or take responsibility for the one social benefit they actually did provide to the public, namely job security on four hours work a day. If you think about it, going from being a backward economy to launching satellites into outer space on four-hour days is pretty impressive. But they could not acknowledge what they were actually giving people. Everybody was pretending to work for eight hours; in fact, they were working four.

It seems that our own societies are beginning to resemble that more and more, as so much work is hollowed from any sort of meaning or point, yet nonetheless people end up feeling obliged, for moral and ideological reasons, to do it more and more. I think a lot of politics can be explained by this. I have always argued that a lot of right-wing populism is based on resentment of people who get to have meaningful jobs. The cultural elite are seen as the people who get to monopolise the jobs where you can actually get paid to do something which is not just for the money. You know, how dare those bastards take all the altruistic jobs?

Similarly, I find fascinating the resentment of autoworkers, or teachers. I think it can only be explained in those sorts of moral terms, that there seems to be a sense that, 'You guys actually get to do something real. You get to teach kids and make cars, you want benefits too?' At any rate, I think that we need to think again about how the kind of morality that money enables, both in terms of debt and work, becomes a driving political force in itself, and that many of the issues that we think of as economic issues are also actually political issues in disguise.

Discussion

Robert Skidelsky

One thing I would be interested to have explained is what causes these cycles of creditor and debtor domination. One group loses power, the other group gains power, and this happens in some alternation. There are obviously creditor interests and there are debtor interests. Farmers have always been classic debtor interests; financiers, bankers and usually exporters credit. What explains the alternation?

David Graeber

I do not actually know. I am trying to describe the process. The best I can say is that there seems to be social mobilisation. You have the rise of these professionalised armies that serve the new social technology, but then you have movements against it. Almost all of the world religions begin as something that we would now think of as peace movements. It is very hard to understand, because a lot of the history has been lost. The one example I always think of here is the end of classical slavery. At the height of the Roman Empire, about 40 per cent of Roman Italy consisted of chattel slaves. That was not true 200 years later. It is one of the great liberations in history, and we do not know how it happened. Christianity clearly had something to do with it.

Robert Skidelsky

This was Perry's point this morning. It is a question of agency: What is it that causes revolts against systems that take the form of popular movements? Catastrophe, but debtors' revolts have been an incredibly powerful motor of history.

David Graeber
I am trying to engineer one right now.

Felix Martin
I offer an answer to Robert's question in my book. It is a different answer to David's, but they are not mutually exclusive. One answer to the question, a realist Marxist one, is to say it is about vested interests. I think, because I am someone who studied economics, that there is also an answer on the level of ideas. If you allow yourself and your system and your policy-makers to be captured by a particular way of thinking about money – thinking of money as a thing, thinking in particular of the monetary standard as a natural fact, something which cannot be legitimately or even possibly manipulated – then one sets up a situation where it becomes almost impossible to have a conversation about manipulating the standard to transfer wealth from creditors to debtors. It no longer makes any sense. You cannot have an ethical discussion about that any more than you can have an ethical discussion about any other feature of the natural world. So I think the problem is on the level of ideas.

Geoffrey Hosking
Can I try another explanation, which is completely different? It seems to me that at a certain stage a massive accumulation of debt ceases to be in the interests of creditors either and they then have to find a way of coping with it. In ancient Greece, creditors enslaved debtors, so you gradually lost your army. That happens in different ways in different societies; nowadays the massive accumulation of debt means in the end that the debtors cannot pay any of their money back and there therefore has to be massive restructuring of debt, but that is what happens eventually.

Robert Skidelsky
Although debt has always been repudiated throughout history – no debts have ever been repaid properly except in trivial cases – we still go on insisting on debtor liability.

Perry Anderson
A lot of it comes back to the question of trust, because what Felix is recommending is debt cancellation by stealth, in effect. That is what inflation does. Of course Geoffrey's story is rather different: it destroys trust if you do that.

Geoffrey Hosking
Hyperinflation certainly does, yes.

Perry Anderson
I was going to ask, do you think that moderate doses of inflation are still trust-preserving, and are preferable to straightforward debt cancellation?

Geoffrey Hosking
Well, it is not only I who think that, it is the IMF, the Treasury, the Bank of England and all the rest of it.

Perry Anderson
You are hiding behind them.

Geoffrey Hosking
It is not just me. A moderate dose of inflation does not destroy trust in the way that hyperinflation does. Obviously there is a long borderland between the two, and it is not possible for me to say at which level inflation destroys trust, but obviously, taken to a high level, it does destroy trust.

Robert Skidelsky
Ten percent is trust-destroying. I think the 1970s is a crucial period in British history when trust really did get

eroded enormously, and the average rate of inflation was about 10 per cent.

Felix Martin
May I defend myself? I am not saying 'by stealth' at all. No, no. These things must be done openly and by a democratic government. As for this question of trust: you are setting up the argument so that it is unwinnable by someone like me. You are taking it as a given of the monetary system that debts must be repaid in real terms, but at some point that becomes politically unsustainable. How can it be to the benefit of trust, how can it build trust in society, that you accumulate a system of debts which is politically unsustainable? This is nonsense.

Geoffrey Hosking
The illusion that you are going to be repaid is certainly trust-generating. After all, some things about trust are illusions, or turn out to be illusions later on. Most creditors resist as long as they can the idea that they are not going to be repaid, and it is only when social tensions reach a very high stage that they eventually accept that at least some debts have to be written off or seriously restructured.

Felix Martin
As Keynes said, the real parents of revolution are the absolutists of contract, and I would say to you that the real destroyers of trust are the absolutists of contract. That is the point.

Robert Skidelsky
One point of the usury laws was to prevent people getting into debts they could not repay. It was a protection for the debtor. Is that not what a whole lot of bank reform, re-regulation and such matters are now designed to do, to actually reduce the lender's premium so you eliminate

the usury elements in interest? You can interpret it all that way, though no central bank governor or Basel chairman has ever put it like that.

Robert H. Frank
The usury laws or the caps on interest rates, I think, have to be understood as attempts to keep people who are vulnerable to easy credit from borrowing beyond their means.

Robert Skidelsky
I agree.

Robert H. Frank
There is a small set in every population such that if money is available – the payday loan industry has been the poster child for this point in the US – money will be lent to them. If you can charge 400 per cent or 500 per cent annually, and some of the payday loan people did, then you can tolerate very high default rates. You can lend to non-creditworthy borrowers and the inevitable outcome of allowing that is that you will have many people forced into bankruptcy by having borrowed beyond any possible limit that they can pay.

Robert Skidelsky
I think it is when an important social group becomes a large-scale debtor that you get social problems. If the group is very limited, then they are dealt with as a sort of sociologically diseased category. But if a big segment of the population gets into debt, then you get a real crisis: a social crisis and an economic crisis. I do not know enough about the history of the usury laws to know how many people were implicated in the usury law structure in the Middle Ages; I mean, how many borrowers were actually protected by the usury laws, how effective the usury laws were, how effective the usury laws in Islam are today.

David Graeber
In Islam, at least in the Middle Ages, they were actually quite effective. People have assumed that everybody ignored them, but recent documentation implies that they did not. It is very interesting, especially because the first real free-market ideology comes out of that period in which usury was effectively eliminated, which allowed people to imagine the market as something which would not need state enforcement. Where you have usury, you pretty much need to shake people down. Hence the idea of relations of trust that can exist entirely outside of governments seems to have been enabled by the elimination of usury.

Notes

1. C.K. Ogden and I.A. Richards, 'The Universal Language', *Psyche*, 9:3 (1929), pp. 1–9.
2. Ibid., p. 9.
3. W.T. Gordon, *C. K. Ogden: A Bio-Bibliographic Study* (London: Scarecrow Press, 1990), p. 48. Most of the details on the spread of Basic English given here are drawn from Gordon's study.
4. L. Carroll, *Through the Looking-Glass, and What Alice Found There* (London: Macmillan,1922 [1871]), p. 124.
5. F. Thom, *Newspeak: The Language of Soviet Communism*, tr. K. Connolly (London: Claridge, 1989), p. 13.
6. The Russian term is *duboviy yazyk* – literally 'language of oak'. It has passed into common usage in French as *la langue du bois*, but for some reason English has no directly analogous expression. Why not is a mystery, since the English language has been subjected to torture at least as merciless by politicians and their spin doctors.
7. G. Orwell *1984* (London: Secker & Warburg 1949).
8. Quoted in Thom, op. cit., p. 18.
9. For Czech official, see Thom, op. cit., p. 28; for abstract nouns, see J.W. Young, *Totalitarian Language: Orwell's Newspeak and its Nazi and Communist Antecedents* (Virginia: University Press of Virginia, 1991), especially pp. 249–50 for list of 'isms'.
10. G. Orwell, 'Politics and the English Language', *Horizon*, April (1946).
11. An example given to Françoise Thom by a translator of the Novosti Press Agency, quoted in Thom, op. cit., p. 52.

12. A. Solzhenitsyn, *The Gulag Archipelago*, quoted in Thom, op. cit., p. 119.
13. Thom, op. cit., pp. 119–20.
14. Ibid., p. 118.
15. V. Klemperer, *LTI: The Language of the Third Reich* (London: Bloomsbury, 2000 [1957]), pp. 15–16.
16. Ibid., p. 10.
17. Ibid.
18. Klemperer explained the former tendency as follows: '*Garant* {guarantor} sounds much more persuasive than *Bürge* {supporter}, and *diffamieren* {defame} far more impressive than *schlechtmachen* {run down}'. As examples of the latter, he gave the *HJ* (*Hitler Jugend* – the Hitler Youth); the *BDM* (*Bund deutscher Madel* – the League of German Girls, the *HJ*'s girls' branch); and the *DAF* (*Deutsche Arbeitsfront* – the German Labour Front, the Nazi trade union organization). Ibid., p. 9.
19. Ibid.
20. Ibid., pp. 9–10.
21. This whole section is taken from Geoffrey Hosking, *Trust: A History*, (Oxford: Oxford University Press, 2014), ch. 4 'Money: Creator and Destroyer of Trust', pp. 81–108, by permission of Oxford University Press.
22. Georg Simmel, *The Philosophy of Money* (London: Routledge, 1978), pp.178–9.
23. Niall Ferguson, *The Ascent of Money: A Financial History of the World* (London: Penguin, 2009), p.21.

Index

Abend, Gabriel 98
Acquisitive individualism 33–4
Addiction to growth 15, 16
Advertising 12, 16, 40–1, 99
Agamben, Giorgio 89
Agency 2, 17–18, 35–6, 37, 39, 53, 55, 94, 137
American Enterprise Institute 32, 37
Anarchism 135
Ancient world 24, 33, 34, 120, 121, 131, 137, 138
Aristotle 10, 11, 14, 74, 88, 131
Aristotelian *teloi* 75, 80, 84, 100–1

Bakunin, Mikhail 135
Bank of England 139
Baumol, William 50–1, 76
Baumol goods 50–1
Beethoven, Ludwig van 50
Berlin, Isaiah 65, 66, 67
Beveridge, William 17, 18
Brahmin theology 126
Buchan, John 9
Buddhism 133

Canetti, Elias 122
Capitalism 14, 88–9
Catholic social teaching 17, 35
Carbon trading 16, 45, 47
Christian democracy 18
Christianity 18, 19, 20, 89–90, 96, 125
Citizenship 51, 53, 55, 69, 72, 79
Coleridge, Samuel Taylor 85
Commodification 46–8, 52, 65
 'fictitious commodification' 52, 85
Conspicuous consumption 12
Comparison 23
 awareness in children 24–5
 between siblings 25
 global 40–41

Corruption 45–52, 56, 59, 77–86
Cruddas, Jon 91

Dante 10
Debt 126–42
 cancellation 127, 133
 relation to power 127
Democracy 56–65, 66, 94
 participation 60
Dworkin, Ronald 63
Dynamism, of monetary societies 34–5, 44

Ecological disaster 19, 40
Economics (as a discipline) 10, 55, 86, 99, 104, 114, 128–9
Economic crash 19, 20, 40, 122
Education 28–9, 71–2, 85
Engels, Friedrich 46
Equality 1, 3, 44–55, 59, 63, 64, 77–8, 127
Exploitation 14, 77

Feminism 54
Ferguson, Niall 121
Financial crisis 9, 67
Finley, Moses 127
First World War 105
Foucault, Michel 89
Franchise *see* voting
Free-rider problems 4, 68–9
Friedman, Milton 32

Galbraith, John Kenneth 12
Gellner, Ernest 20
Genovesi, Antonio 93
Gibbon, Edward 11
Gift exchange 87, 88
Ginsborg, Paul 20
Goethe, Johann Wolfgang von 13
Great Depression 18

145

Index

Happiness/wellbeing 15, 16
Harm, intrinsic *v.* aggravating 45, 53–4, 69–70
Hart, Keith 129
Healthcare *see* medical services
Hirsch, Fred 28, 42
Housing 31
'How am I doing?' question 25
How Much Is Enough? 1, 8, 15, 17, 19–20, 32, 86
Human flourishing 48, 91
Hyperinflation 114, 115, 121, 139

Identity 54, 65
Illich, Ivan 89, 90
Incomes 2, 8, 15, 38, 41–42, 117
Inequality 16, 21, 53–5, 127–8
  of income 41
  relative 27–8
Innes, Alfred Mitchell 103
Insatiability 8–15
Internal goals (*see also* Aristotelian *teloi*) 59, 79
International Monetary Fund 133, 139
Islam 10, 124, 141–2

Jansenism 90
Jaspers, Karl 129
Jevons, William Stanley 11–12

Kant, Immanuel 66
Keynes, John Maynard 8, 14, 15, 16, 17, 18, 21, 96
Klemperer, Viktor 111–13

Labour 13, 18
  movements 18
Language 105–13
  Basic English 105–7
  in *1984* 111
  LTI 112
  totalitarian 108–14
Latour, Bruno 91
Layard, Richard 30

Libertarianism 21, 69
Love of goods 9, 13, 17

MacIntyre, Alasdair 17
Mandeville, Bernard de 90
Marginal utility 9, 13
Marginalism 91, 92
Markets 44–55, 55–65, 77, 86–95, 96
  distinction between markets and marketplace 86–7
  in voting 56–65
Marr, N.J. 108
Marshall, T.H. 55
Marx, Karl 13, 14, 16, 46, 74, 88, 92, 95, 124, 135
Marxism 40, 72, 88, 135–6
Medical services 49, 51, 59–60, 74–6, 80, 84
Meikle, Scott 74
Mencken, H.L. 25
Michéa, Jean-Claude 90
Middle classes 19–20
Midas 8, 9
Monetary policy 67
Money 103–17, 118–25
  and trust 118125
  as a unit of account 114, 129
  as a moral technology 125–37
  as a social technology 116, 137
  as a symbolic system 123–5
  coinage 120–1, 130
  credit 10
  fiat/credit money *v.* commodity money 9, 128–9, 130, 132–3
  inflation 116–17, 139
  love of money 8, 9, 15, 16
  monetary standard 113–15, 138
  pre-monetary society 33, 119
  private money 114
Monopsony 62
Montaigne, Michel de 81, 83
Morris, William 85
Murphy, Thomas 85

Index

Nagel, Thomas 82
Needs . wants 22
New Liberalism 17, 18
Novelty, psychological addiction to 12, 13
Nozick, Robert 59–60, 65

Oakeshott, Michael 64
Ogden, C.K. 105
Oikonomia 89
Organ transplant 53
Orwell, George 108–11

Pareto principle 58, 59, 79
Pleasures, higher and lower 12
Pluralism 67
Polanyi, Karl 52, 85, 87–8, 94
Polygamy 29
Positional goods 28, 42
Posner, Richard 26
Productivity growth 8
Prostitution 53–5, 77–86, 100–2
Provoost, Jan 123
Public service broadcasting 51–2

Radin, Margaret 45, 46, 49
Rational choice Rawls, John 63
Relative advantage 29
Relative wants 12
Religious resurgence 19, 35–6, 40
Revealed preference theory 58
Richards, I.A. 105
Rights 55
Roosevelt, Franklin Delano 17, 18
Routes nationales 50, 67
Ruskin, John 85
Russell, Robert 57, 64

Same-sex marriage 36, 37
Samuelson, Paul 71, 103
Sandel, Michael 44, 46–8, 56, 59, 61, 64, 69, 79
Sartre, Jean-Paul 81
Satz, Deborah 44, 48, 53–5, 57, 61, 64, 78–9, 83

Schelling, Thomas 53, 66
'Schmoctering' 59–60, 73–74, 80
Schopenhauer, Arthur 9
Schumpeter, Joseph 96
Scitovsky, Tibor 12, 34
Simmel, Georg 124
Second World War 18, 32, 67, 111
Self-objectification 82
Sex 53–5, 77–86, 100–2
 telos of 80–4, 100–1
Shakespeare, William 14
Smith, Adam 10, 11, 24, 34, 90, 92
Social benefit 95
Socialism 92–4
Stalin, Josef 108

Tax 15
 consumption 15, 31–2, 36–8
 income 16
Thom, Francoise 110
Totalitarianism 108–13, 114
Transformation 17–19
Trust 96, 117–25, 139–42
 thin *v*. thick trust 118

Universal basic income 16
Usury 10, 45, 124, 131, 132, 140–2
Utilitarianism 65, 91, 99, 132
UK 18, 21, 51, 64, 65, 116
USA 21, 24, 29, 31, 32, 36–7, 50, 51–52, 58, 65, 72, 75, 106, 121, 131, 134
USSR 105, 108–10, 135

Value 1, 4, 6, 14, 27, 34, 40, 42, 46–7, 50, 57, 61–9, 85, 87–8, 91, 103–4, 114, 117, 119–24, 134
 commensurability 46, 65–7, 72–3, 97, 104
 moral values 1, 87–8
Veblen, Thorsten 12, 13
Vico, Giambattista 93
Voting 56–65
 compulsory voting 60

Weber, Max 73
Welfare state 21
Wilde, Oscar 124
Williams, Bernard 59

Woolf, Virginia 96
Working hours 15, 16, 134–6

Zelizer, Viviana 48, 50, 71

GPSR Compliance

The European Union's (EU) General Product Safety Regulation (GPSR) is a set of rules that requires consumer products to be safe and our obligations to ensure this.

If you have any concerns about our products, you can contact us on

ProductSafety@springernature.com

In case Publisher is established outside the EU, the EU authorized representative is:

Springer Nature Customer Service Center GmbH
Europaplatz 3
69115 Heidelberg, Germany

www.ingramcontent.com/pod-product-compliance
Lightning Source LLC
Chambersburg PA
CBHW071703100426
42873CB00017B/400